THE
KINGFISHER
FACTS
AND
RECORDS
BOOK

Deputy Art Director   Mike Buckley
Art Editor   Keith Davis
Designer   Joe Conneally

Editors   Fergus Collins, Jonathan Stroud
Editorial Assistant   Robert Cave

Picture Researcher   Tara McCormack

DTP Co-ordinator   Nicky Studdart

Production Controller   Jacquie Horner

Artwork Archivists   Wendy Allison, Steve Robinson

Indexer   Sue Lightfoot

KINGFISHER
Kingfisher Publications Plc
New Penderel House,
283–288 High Holborn,
London WC1V 7HZ

Produced by Scintilla Editorial
33 Great Portland Street,
London WIN 5DD

First published by Kingfisher Publications Plc 2000
1 3 5 7 9 10 8 6 4 2
1TR/0400/TWP/HBM(MNA)/150ARM

A CIP catalogue record for this book is available from the British Library.

ISBN 0 7534 0434 6

Printed in Singapore

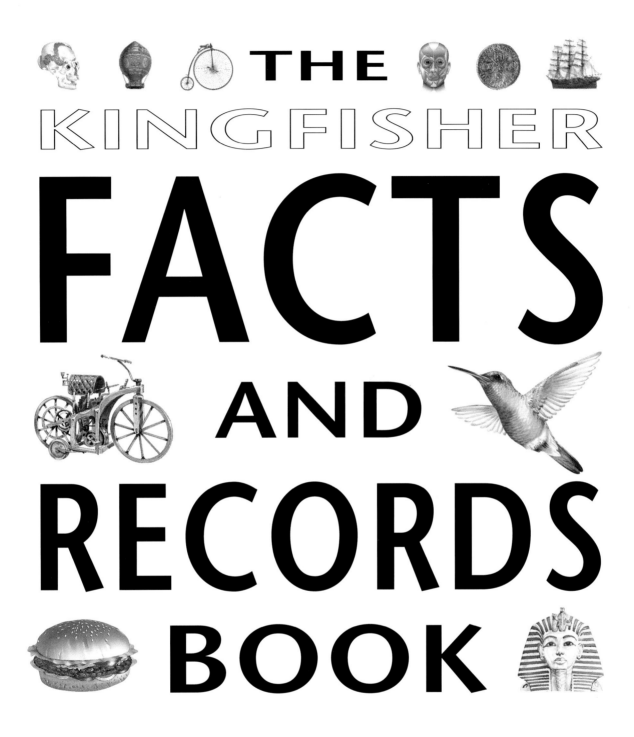

THE KINGFISHER FACTS AND RECORDS BOOK

KING*f*ISHER

INTRODUCTION

Welcome to *The Kingfisher Facts and Records Book*! In the following pages you will find a huge amount of intriguing information on a staggering variety of subjects. It is divided into 11 fact-filled sections, which give exciting insights into everything from space to cinema and from nature to art.

INVENTIONS!
Learn about amazing inventions, such as this early submarine. It was used by the Americans against Britain during the American War of Independence (1775–80).

The Kingfisher Facts and Records Book is an exploration and celebration of our incredible world and the achievements of its many remarkable people. As well as examining Earth and its natural wonders, the book highlights key discoveries, crucial moments in history and great human feats.

RICHES!
Discover the most precious objects on Earth, such as the British Crown Jewels. Read about the largest diamond ever discovered and the most expensive bottle of wine!

Discover who made the first space explorations; which pop artist has sold the most albums; how many times we breathe in our lives; which is the world's tallest building; how soccer began; which is the oldest tree... and many more.

BIZARRE FACTS!
Did you know that in Australia goods lorries with several long trailers take the place of trains for transporting freight?

SOLAR SYSTEM

The Solar System is made up of the Sun and its nine orbiting planets. The Sun exerts a huge gravitational pull on the planets, preventing them from drifting away.

The Sun

The Sun is really a small star. It is 30,000 times heavier than Earth and has a diameter of 1.4 million km. Nuclear reactions at its core produce immense heat and light. The temperature is 15 million°C at the core, but only 6000°C on the surface – still 24 times as hot as a typical oven. It uses 4–7 million tonnes of fuel a second and yet is so vast that all the fuel it has ever used equals only 0.01 per cent of its original weight when it began shining 5 billion years ago.

Core

Radiative zone

Convective zone

Photosphere – the Sun's surface

The planets

The nine planets range in size from tiny Pluto, which is smaller than Earth's Moon, to Jupiter, which has a diameter 11 times greater than Earth. Mercury, Venus, Earth and Mars, the inner planets, are small rocky worlds. Jupiter, Saturn, Uranus and Neptune are huge and consist of gas, liquid and ice. Little is known about cold and remote Pluto at the outer edge of the Solar System. Some scientists believe that there is a tenth planet beyond Pluto still to be discovered – Planet X.

Venus takes longer to spin on its axis than to orbit the Sun – so its days are longer than its years.

CHARON
Pluto is twice the size of its moon, Charon. Pluto was located in 1930 but Charon was only discovered in 1978.

MERCURY
Distance from Sun: 57.9 million km
Diameter: 4,878km
Day: 58 days 14 hrs
Year: 88 days

VENUS
Distance from Sun: 108.2 million km
Diameter: 12,104km
Day: 244 days
Year: 225 days

EARTH
Distance from Sun: 149.6 million km
Diameter: 12,756km
Day: 24 hrs
Year: 365 days

Measurements in Earth days and years. Distance from Sun is average.

VOYAGER I & II
Launched in 1979, two identical probes were used to explore Saturn. *Voyager II* went on to the outer planets.

GAS GIANT
Saturn is made up of swirling gases, such as hydrogen and helium. Its 23 moons, however, are mostly rocky.

RINGS
Saturn's rings are not solid, but are made up of billions of pieces of rocky debris that orbit the planet.

Probing the planets

Little would be known about the planets without space probes. These unmanned craft, such as *Pioneer*, have visited every planet except Pluto. In 1997, *Mars Pathfinder* landed on Mars. It carried a remote-controlled vehicle, which scientists on Earth used to examine the planet's surface. The probe *Voyager 1*, launched in 1977, visited Jupiter and Saturn. It has now left the Solar System and in 1998 was 10.4 billion km from Earth – the remotest man-made object ever. Probes are today's great explorers of the unknown and each year they reveal more about the mysteries of space.

Until the 16th century, most people thought that the Sun and its planets revolved around the Earth.

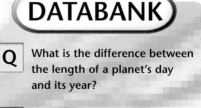

DATABANK

Q What is the difference between the length of a planet's day and its year?

A A day is the time a planet takes to rotate once. A year is how long it takes to orbit the Sun.

Q What is the huge red spot that can be seen regularly passing across the surface of Jupiter?

A It is a storm 40,000km in diameter that has been raging for at least 300 years.

MARS
Distance from Sun: 227.9 million km
Diameter: 6,794km
Day: 24.5 hrs
Year: 687 days

JUPITER
Distance from Sun: 778.3 million km
Diameter: 142,800km
Day: 9 hrs 55 mins
Year: 11 years, 314 days

SATURN
Distance from Sun: 1,430 million km
Diameter: 120,000km
Day: 10 hrs 40 mins
Year: 29 years, 168 days

URANUS
Distance from Sun: 2,870 million km
Diameter: 51,000km
Day: 17 hrs 15 mins
Year: 84 years, 4 days

NEPTUNE
Distance from Sun: 4,500 million km
Diameter: 49,500km
Day: 16 hrs 7 mins
Year: 164 years, 298 days

PLUTO
Distance from Sun: 5,900 million km
Diameter: 2,300km
Day: 6 days 9 hrs
Year: 247 years, 256 days

DEEPER SPACE

Little is known about deepest space. Scientists are keen to find out more about galaxies, stars and black holes so that they can develop a better understanding of the Universe, Earth and the origins of life itself.

Big bang

There are many ideas about how the Universe was created, but most scientists now think it started with the 'Big Bang'. They believe the Universe once fitted into a tiny ball the size of a pinhead. This ball then exploded and released all the matter that now makes up the Universe. Scientists still argue about how the Universe will end. Some believe it will go on expanding forever; others think it could reach a point at which it starts to contract into a tiny ball again. We should not worry, though, as it will take billions of years to happen!

A light year is the distance that light travels in a year. Light travels at a speed of 300,000 km/sec.

Our Solar System is 12 light hours – not light years – wide, so it is small compared to a galaxy.

EINSTEIN
Albert Einstein's General Theory of Relativity, published in 1915, shows how time and space are linked. It provides the framework for our modern ideas about the Universe.

SCORCHER
After the Big Bang, it took over 300,000 years for the Universe to cool enough for the first atoms to form.

EXPANDING UNIVERSE
Galaxies began to form 1.4 million years after the Big Bang. The Universe is still expanding 14 billion years later.

DEEP FIELD SCAN
In 1995, the *Hubble* Space Telescope spotted 1,500 galaxies during a 10-day scan of a single stretch of sky.

DATABANK

INPUT	OUTPUT
Q How wide is the Milky Way?	**A** The main part of the Milky Way is 75,000 light years wide.
Q Do stars move in space?	**A** Yes, our Solar System orbits the galaxy every 200 million years.
Q How does the *Hubble* Space Telescope work?	**A** As it is an unmanned satellite, it radios its findings back to Earth.
Q How hot is it at the centre of a supernova?	**A** Some scientists estimate that it may be 5,000 million°C.

Stars and black holes

Stars vary widely in size and brightness. Our Sun is small compared with giants like Betelgeuse, whose diameter is 700 times as large. All stars are born in massive clouds of debris called nebulas. Here, gravity eventually pulls the debris so tightly together that a nuclear reaction takes place, emitting light and heat – a star is born! When a star runs out of fuel at the end of its life, a number of things can happen. A star the size of our Sun or smaller will eventually shrink and cool. Larger stars explode spectacularly as supernovas, their remains forming a nebula. If the star is more than five times the size of our Sun, the star's core could collapse upon itself to form a black hole.

Black holes are not really holes, but solid spherical objects that attract objects from all directions.

NO ESCAPE
The dark area at the centre of a black hole is called the event horizon. Not even light can evade its grasp.

DRAINING AWAY
A nearby star is powerless to prevent its material from being sucked away by the pull of the black hole's massive gravity.

Galaxies

A galaxy contains millions of stars, bound together with gases and dust by their gravitational pull towards each other. The Sun is just one of the 200 billion stars in our own galaxy, the Milky Way. The Milky Way resembles a spiral-shaped disk with a bright bulging cloud at its centre. This cloud is so bright that we cannot see what lies at its centre, but some scientists believe that it could be hiding a black hole. There are uncounted millions of galaxies in the Universe and they take many different shapes. Some resemble spirals or balls, others are more irregular, resembling misty clouds. In 1937, Clyde Tombaugh, who also located the planet Pluto, discovered that galaxies themselves are arranged into clusters.

A pulsar is a rapidly rotating star that spins faster than a washing machine – up to 622 times a second.

STAR SPIRAL
At 2,200,000 light years from Earth, the Andromeda spiral galaxy may contain as many as 400 billion stars.

FACTS AND FIGURES

The nearest galaxy to our own is Magellan, which is over 150,000 light years away.

700 baby stars have been seen in the Orion Nebula, a cloud of matter where stars form.

Proxima Centauri is the nearest star to our Sun. It is 40,000 billion km away.

The Earth is roughly 30,000 light years away from the centre of the Milky Way.

The Crab Nebula is the remnant of a supernova that the Chinese saw in AD1054.

PEOPLE IN SPACE

Even before the 20th century, people dreamed of travelling beyond the Earth's atmosphere and exploring space. But it was not until rocket technology was developed during World War II (1939–45) that such fantasies could be turned into reality.

The space race

In the 1950s, 60s and 70s, Russia and the USA were the only countries wealthy enough to build space rockets. However, because of differing political beliefs, the two countries did not trust each other. Instead of co-operating, they competed fiercely. The Russians led the way by sending the first satellite into space in 1957. In the same year they also sent the first animal into orbit – a fox terrier called Laika on board the spacecraft *Sputnik 2*. On 12 April 1961, the Russian cosmonaut Major Yuri Gagarin made history in the *Vostok* spaceship by becoming the first man in space. After orbiting the Earth once, he made a safe landing back on the ground. In 1962, John Glenn became the first American to reach orbit. After several more space flights, Russia and America turned their attention to the greatest goal of all – the Moon.

From 1959 to 1976 there were 48 Russian and 31 American unmanned Moon missions. About half failed.

YURI GAGARIN
Having survived his epic trip into space, Gagarin became a global hero. He was killed in a plane crash in 1968.

There is no wind or atmosphere on the Moon. Astronauts' footprints will remain unchanged forever.

SATURN V
Used on Moon missions, this huge rocket was 110m tall – equalling the height of St Paul's Cathedral in London, UK.

DATABANK

INPUT	OUTPUT
Q How many people have walked on the Moon's surface?	**A** 12, all American. The Russians abandoned manned Moon flights.
Q How long would it take to travel by space rocket to Mars?	**A** It would take up to a year to travel the 78 million km to Mars.
Q Who was the first woman to be sent into space?	**A** The Russian Valentina Tereshkova visited space in 1963.
Q Why did the Space Shuttle *Challenger* explode in 1986?	**A** Frost before take-off weakened seals on the fuel tank.

THE FUTURE
Some asteroids are made of metals, such as iron. Eventually it may be possible to drag them into Earth's orbit to be mined.

SPACE POWER
One day, solar power collectors may be able to beam the Sun's energy to Earth to generate electricity.

Giant leap

The Americans were determined to be the first to put a man on the Moon. In 1969, after a series of test flights, the Saturn V rocket *Apollo 11* set out on this ultimate mission. On 20 July, while the command module orbited the Moon, the landing craft, named *Eagle*, detached itself with Buzz Aldrin and Neil Armstrong inside. After a risky descent, *Eagle* landed on a flat plain. Finally, in front of a television audience of millions, Armstrong, followed by Aldrin, stepped out of the *Eagle* to explore the alien landscape. For the space agency, NASA, it was a triumph and prompted worldwide celebrations.

Despite several fatal accidents in Earth's atmosphere, no astronauts have yet been killed in space.

MOON BUGGY
Made from light aluminium, the lunar rover was used to explore large areas of the Moon's rocky surface.

Space stations

While the Americans continued to visit the Moon in the early 1970s, the Russians built space stations to be used as orbiting laboratories. The first of these were the *Salyuts* but they were replaced by *Mir* in 1986. This was still in use in the late 1990s. The Americans responded with *Skylab* space station in 1974 and later with the Space Shuttle, which has since been used to put satellites into orbit and conduct experiments in space. In the 1990s, the Americans and Russians have co-operated on the multinational space station *Freedom*, which will be completed soon after the year 2000. There are also plans to revisit the Moon and build a permanent base there.

The Space Shuttle is a reusable spacecraft. The first shuttle, *Columbia*, took off in 1981.

FACTS AND FIGURES

Rockets must travel at a speed of 11 km/sec to pull clear of the Earth's gravity.

The longest stay in space is 437 days 18 hours by Russian Valeri Polyakov.

The first space walk was performed by Russian Aleksey Leonov in 1965.

In 1998, John Glenn, aged 77, became the oldest man to visit space.

The Apollo programme returned just under 300kg of Moon rock to the Earth.

The first docking between US and Russian spacecraft occurred in 1975.

SKY WATCHING

The night sky has long been a source of wonder. Some people saw images of gods in the stars, while others used the night sky to predict the future – but all have felt a sense of awe.

Astronomers

People have probably studied the stars since prehistoric times, but it was in 2000BC that the Ancient Babylonians began to name groups, or constellations, of stars. Later, the Chinese and Egyptians used the stars to develop calendars that could predict the changing seasons. Astronomy was revolutionized in 1609, when Galileo Galilei adapted the newly invented telescope for sky watching. He made detailed observations of the Moon and discovered some of Jupiter's moons. Astronomers used telescopes to map the night sky and, later, split their maps into two to compare the night skies in the Northern and Southern Hemispheres.

Shooting stars are particles of dust that burn up brightly as they enter Earth's atmosphere.

ASTRONOMER
Egyptian star-gazer, Ptolemy, (AD90–168) used Babylonian star charts to explain his theories of the Universe.

SPACE CRATER
Space objects can strike Earth. 50,000 years ago this meteorite hit Arizona, USA. It left a crater 1.2km wide.

Pegasus

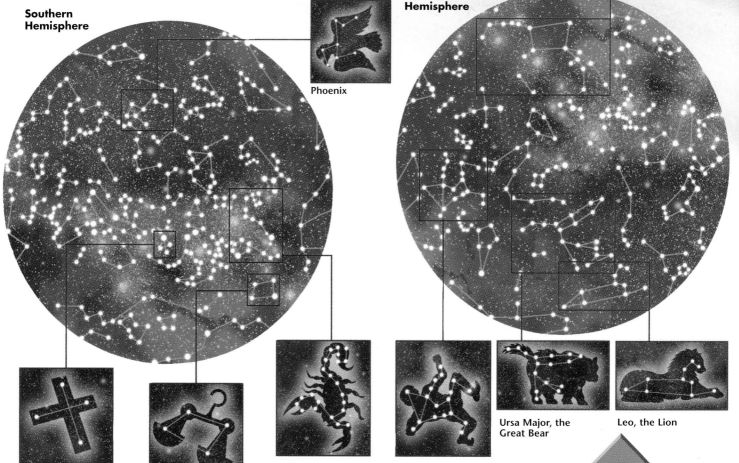

Southern Hemisphere

Northern Hemisphere

Phoenix

The Southern Cross

Libra, the Scales

Scorpius, the Scorpion

Hercules

Ursa Major, the Great Bear

Leo, the Lion

MAPS OF THE STARS
Stars seen from Earth are grouped into constellations. People in the south have a different star map to those in the north.

FACTS AND FIGURES

Halley's Comet was discovered by Edmund Halley in 1682. It orbits Earth every 76 years.

The brightest star in the night sky is Sirius, sometimes known as the Dog Star.

The most frequently seen comet is called Encke. It orbits Earth every three years.

Tycho Brahe (1546–1601) charted 777 stars using his unaided eyesight alone.

Keck Telescopes I and II are the largest on Earth, with apertures of 10.86m.

The Great Comet of 1863 had the longest tail recorded, stretching 800 million km.

COMET'S ICY CORE
The head of a comet is only a few kilometres wide, but its tail of vapourized ice may be millions of kilometres long.

Comets

A comet is a lump of ice in orbit around the Sun. Its characteristic tail forms as it melts with the Sun's heat. In the past, people thought that comets were omens of good or evil. Halley's Comet appears in the Bayeux Tapestry as a warning of William the Conqueror's victory at the Battle of Hastings in England in 1066. Today, scientists believe that comets come from the Oort Cloud, a cluster of billions of objects outside the orbit of the planet Pluto.

William Herschel was the first man to discover a planet by telescope, when he located Uranus in 1781.

Solar eclipses

At least twice a year, the Moon's orbit places it between Earth and the Sun, preventing some sunlight reaching us. This event is called a solar eclipse and can be seen in one of three ways. A partial eclipse occurs when only part of the Moon's shadow, or penumbra, is seen from Earth. An annular eclipse occurs when the Moon is at its farthest point from Earth and does not appear big enough to cover the Sun. By far the most exciting, a total eclipse, occurs when the Moon entirely covers the Sun. Those directly beneath experience a period of almost 'night-time' darkness in the middle of the day.

During a total eclipse, the wind drops and animals become eerily quiet in anticipation of nightfall.

DATABANK

Q What causes the strange lights in the sky known as the *Aurora Borealis* and *Aurora Australis*?

A These lights are caused by the Sun's radiation striking Earth's atmosphere at the two poles.

Q What's the difference between an asteroid and a meteor?

A An asteroid is a rock that orbits the Sun. A meteor is a rock that enters Earth's atmosphere.

IN THE MOON'S SHADOW
In a total eclipse, the darkest area, or umbra, is only 150km wide and sweeps across the surface as the Earth rotates.

VIOLENT EARTH

Earth is the only planet in our solar system capable of sustaining life, yet it is still a volatile place. Volcanoes burst through its delicate crust and earthquakes regularly shake the land.

Crust: 5–35km thick

Mantle: 2,900km thick

Outer core: 2,200km thick

Inner core: 1,200km thick

Fragile crust

Earth's crust is only 5km thick in places and is divided into pieces, known as continental plates. Molten rock swirls beneath the crust, reaching 6300°C at the Earth's core. Under pressure, the rock forces itself through weaknesses in the crust, particularly along the edges of the plates. The movement of molten rock causes the plates to crash together or drift apart, causing volcanoes and earthquakes. Two famous areas of plate activity are the Rift Valley in Africa and the San Andreas Fault in North America.

Continental plates move at the same rate that fingernails grow – about 5–10cm a year.

WAFER THIN
The Earth's crust is incredibly thin compared to the immensely thick layers of molten rock beneath – like the outer skin of an onion compared to the rest of the vegetable.

Shaken and stirred

As continental plates grind against each other, enormous pressure builds up until the ground suddenly buckles, causing an earthquake. Waves of energy flow through the ground, and can flatten entire cities. Scientists measure these 'seismic' waves on the Richter scale as a number from zero up to 10. One of the most powerful earthquakes occurred in Alaska in 1964. It measured 9.2 on the Richter scale but caused few deaths as the area was sparsely populated. Earthquakes near or beneath the sea may create huge waves, called tsunamis. Reaching heights of 50m and speeds of 900 km/h, these walls of water are unstoppable. In 1896, in Honshu, Japan, 26,000 people were killed by a tsunami.

ALL SHOOK UP
The Mercalli Scale measures an earthquake's damage. It ranges from I (gentle tremor) to XII (total destruction).

FACTS AND FIGURES

The Krakatau eruption of 1883 was heard 2,200km away in Australia.

The Krakatau eruption also created a tsunami 35m high, ravaging nearby coasts.

The longest earthquake on record occurred in Alaska in 1964. It lasted four minutes.

In 1815, the Tambora volcano in Indonesia may have killed 90,000 people.

The earthquake in Kobe, Japan, in 1995, caused over $100 billion worth of damage.

Aconcagua in Argentina is the world's tallest volcano. It is 6,960m high.

The 1976 earthquake at Tangshan in China killed over 240,000 people.

Volcanic activity began at Kilauea in Hawaii in 1790 and has continued ever since.

Volcanoes

Some volcanoes ooze rivers of molten lava, which flow at up to 5 km/h. When these occur on the seabed, the lava cools and hardens in the water and other layers pile on top. These eventually reach such a height that an island is created. The Hawaiian islands were formed in this way, as was Surtsey, which appeared off the coast of Iceland in 1963. Other eruptions, such as Tambora in 1815 and Krakatau in 1883, are much more violent. Pressure builds up causing explosions, which eject ash, showers of rocks and poisonous gases.

The Krakatau eruption created a gigantic tsunami that carried a ship 2.6km up a river.

HOT STUFF
When Mount Pelée erupted in 1902, searing hot gas and ash wiped out the port of St Pierre, in Martinique.

PRIMEVAL FORCE
In 1980, Mount St Helens in the USA erupted violently, destroying 250 homes and killing 57 people.

BLAST FROM THE PAST
In AD79, Mount Vesuvius, Italy, suddenly erupted, covering Pompeii in ash. The people had little chance of escape.

DOOM RIVER
Liquid lava from a volcano is around 1000°C, hot enough to burn anything in its way. It can also travel at great speed. As it cools, lava hardens into solid rock and turns black.

LAND AND SEA

Earth is a planet of great contrasts. Most of its surface is covered with vast oceans that teem with life, yet large tracts of land are barren deserts. To cap it all, the two poles are frozen, inhospitable wildernesses.

Oceans

About 71 per cent of Earth's surface is covered with water and 97 per cent of this is found in the oceans. Close to land, the water is shallow and fertile and supports most of the life to be found in the oceans. Farther out, oceans can become very deep. The Marianas Trench in the Pacific Ocean descends 11,034m below sea level – the deepest water on Earth. The water pressure at the seabed is too great for humans to survive without specially adapted submarines, and so most of the ocean floor remains unexplored.

Tides are caused by the gravitational pull of the Sun and Moon on the seas and oceans.

OCEAN BLUE
The Atlantic Ocean (top) is 106 million km². However, it is small compared to the Pacific Ocean (above). This covers 180 million km² and could fit all the world's land within it.

SEABED
Plants, such as seaweed, survive only in shallow coastal areas where sunlight penetrates to the seabed.

Shallow waters close to land support many plants, fish and other creatures.

Mid-ocean ridges are undersea mountain ranges.

The average depth of the oceans is 3,500m.

Deep ocean trenches are home to strange fish, molluscs and crustaceans.

Volcanoes under the sea sometimes build up to form islands.

JUST ABOUT BEAR-ABLE
Many animals, big and small, visit the Arctic in summer to feed. In winter, they travel to warmer areas farther south.

Icy wastes

Nowhere on Earth is as cold and barren as the North and South poles. The Arctic, in the north, is a frozen ocean; the Antarctic, in the south, is a huge continent of which 98 per cent is covered in ice up to 4,000m thick. It is the coldest place on Earth with average winter temperatures of –60°C, so few animals live there. The Arctic is warmer, reaching –40°C in winter. In summer, large parts of the polar ice sheet break off, forming icebergs.

EVEREST
The world's tallest mountain soars 8,863m above sea level. It has claimed the lives of many climbers.

VERTICAL VISTA
The Grand Canyon is the world's largest gorge. Its steep walls were carved out by the Colorado River, which flows along it.

High and low

A mountain range is formed when huge rocks are forced upwards as a result of a collision between sections of the Earth's crust known as plates. The highest mountain range, the Himalayas, is growing taller every year as the Indian plate pushes into the Asian plate. The world's longest mountain chain is the Andes, which runs for 7,200km through South America. Even as mountains rise up, the forces of erosion, such as wind and water, are wearing them down. Over time, water and ice flowing down the mountainsides carve out valleys.

The top of the valley is eroded into a circular shape.

The glacier picks up rock debris as it moves.

Just deserts

Deserts are dry areas with little rainfall or plant life. They cover a third of the world's land and include the Kalahari in southern Africa and the Arabian Desert in the Middle East. The largest desert is the Sahara in Africa, which covers 9 million km². In the hottest months of the year, the temperature reaches a maximum of 58°C. Saharan animals need special adaptations to survive this heat.

Although it is covered in ice, the Antarctic is a desert because little rain falls and the air is very dry.

GLACIER
A glacier is a huge body of ice that slowly slides down a mountainside, gouging out a U-shaped valley as it does so. Glaciers move very slowly – by only a few metres a year.

FACTS AND FIGURES

The coldest temperature ever recorded on Earth was –89°C logged in Antarctica in 1983.

Lambert Glacier, in the Antarctic, is the world's largest – 700km long.

Mont Blanc is the tallest mountain in Europe. It is just over half the size of Everest.

ENVIRONMENT

The environment is the world around us, including the land, sea and air and all the plants and animals that share the planet. Everything exists together in a delicate balance. The actions of humans are starting to affect this balance, with potentially devastating consequences for the future.

Climate: a warmer world

The term 'climate' refers to a region's usual weather: hot and dry, or cold and rainy, for instance. It is determined by the region's nearness to the equator and the prevailing winds, but even the oceans and forests have an effect. Records show that Earth's overall climate has been getting warmer since the 17th century, when the industrial age began. This 'global warming' increases the risk of severe weather conditions, such as floods, drought and hurricanes.

Global warming is melting the ice caps at the two poles and raising the level of the world's oceans.

FORESTS
Over 14 per cent of Brazil's rainforest (equal to an area the size of France) has been cut down to provide grazing land for cattle and wood for industry. This destruction is increasing.

Greenhouse effect

Earth is surrounded by a layer of gases – the atmosphere. This acts like a greenhouse, letting sunlight in but stopping some of the Sun's heat from escaping back into space. It keeps Earth warm enough for life. Most of the gas is carbon dioxide (CO_2), which is produced by animals and by burning fossil fuels, such as coal and oil. Todays, scientists are worried that we produce far too much CO_2, which adds to global warming.

OZONE HOLE
The ozone layer, which keeps out cancer-causing solar rays, is being destroyed by gases from some spray cans.

KILLER RAIN
Many trees are killed by acid rain, which forms when gases from cars and power stations mix with water in the clouds.

FACTS AND FIGURES

Wood pulp, for making paper and building materials, uses up four billion trees a year.

Worldwide, over 15,000 species of plants and animals are at risk of extinction.

In 1984, 2,500 people died after toxic gas leaked from a factory in Bhopal, India.

The USA is the biggest user of paper in the world – 67 million tonnes each year.

Living planet

In 1979, UK scientist James Lovelock proposed the Gaia theory. In this he claimed that Earth's living matter, air, oceans and land interact with each other, which keeps the planet a fit place for life. Trees are an example of this. They take in water from the soil and release it from their leaves, from where it forms clouds and falls as rain. They also absorb the waste gas carbon dioxide (CO_2) from the air and release oxygen, which every animal needs in order to live. Humans disrupt this delicate process. Clearing rainforests limits the number of trees that absorb CO_2, which then builds up and adds to global warming. Fewer trees also means less rainfall and so areas of fertile land become dry, hostile desert.

OIL SPILLS
Every year, leaks from oil tankers and pipelines kill thousands of seabirds and other forms of marine life. Major oil spills can devastate coastal habitats and important fishing grounds.

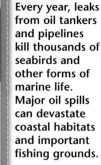

In some parts of the world, huge sails harness the power of the wind to produce electricity.

A greener future

Many governments are now taking steps to protect the environment. We can all help by becoming energy efficient: insulating our homes, for example, means less energy is wasted. Instead of burning fossil fuels, more of our energy needs could be met by non-polluting forms, such as solar, wind and wave power. Recycling paper, tin, wood and plastic preserves natural resources. Trees can be planted to replace those that are lost, and we can help protect wildlife habitats.

SOLAR ENERGY
One day, cars may be fuelled by energy from solar panels, which make electricity from sunlight – without pollution.

DATABANK

INPUT	OUTPUT
Q Which oil spill has had the worst effect on the environment?	**A** The *Exxon Valdez* oil spill of 1989 ruined much of Alaska's coast.
Q Which country in the West recycles the most waste?	**A** Holland recycles over 50% of its paper, and 60% of its glass.
Q Where was the world's worst air pollution disaster?	**A** In Indonesia, in 1997. Forest-burning caused record levels of smog.
Q Which European country has suffered most from acid rain?	**A** Germany. Over 51% of its forests have been damaged.

FOREST LOSS
In the clouds, pollution gases are turned into sulphuric and nitric acid. This falls as rain, polluting lakes and destroying huge areas of forest in Europe and North America.

WEATHER

Come sunshine, snow, wind or rain, the weather affects every day of our lives. In some parts of the world, severe weather is a regular threat to life.

Forecasting

Weather forecasting is vital. Ships' captains need to know when it is safe to sail, for instance, and farmers must be told when tender crops need protection. Weather is determined by many factors, including humidity, temperature and wind, which makes it very difficult to predict. Before the 20th century, forecasting mostly relied on folklore, but it has now become a science. Thousands of measurements are taken from weather stations on the ground and satellites in space in order to spot changes in the weather. Even so, forecasts are not always accurate.

Roy Sullivan from Virginia, USA, was struck by lightning seven times during his life.

CHARTS
Lines of triangles on weather maps indicate cold air. Lines of semi-circles indicate warm air. They are called fronts.

TWISTER
A tornado is like a concentrated hurricane, often only 400m wide. It appears with little warning and causes much damage. The winds inside a tornado have been measured at 450 km/h.

Raining again...

A cloud is a vast accumulation of water droplets, drawn up as vapour from plants, rivers and oceans. As water builds up in the cloud, the droplets grow until they are too heavy to stay up in the sky and so fall as rain. The rainy season in southeast Asia is called the monsoon. In some areas, such as Bangladesh and parts of China, this heavy, sustained downpour often floods vast areas of low-lying land, drowning many people. Rain may be accompanied by a thunderstorm. This is caused by a huge build-up of electricity in the rain clouds, which is released as a series of high-voltage flashes, seen as lightning. As sound travels more slowly than light, the noise of these flashes, which is known as thunder, is heard seconds later.

SKY-HIGH VOLTAGE
When a flash of lightning strikes the ground, a return stroke is sent back from the ground to the cloud instantly.

BLOW ME DOWN
Tornadoes are unpredictable. The funnel of air suddenly touches the ground without warning, destroying homes.

FACTS AND FIGURES

SUCKING UP
Tornadoes are very common in central and southeastern USA. Some are strong enough to suck up very large objects, such as cars. A freezer was once carried for 2km by a tornado.

A tornado that hit Shaturia in Bangladesh in 1989 left 1,300 dead and 50,000 homeless.

A typhoon that struck Hong Kong in 1906 may have killed as many as 10,000 people.

The world's worst hailstorm occurred in India in 1988 and killed 246 people.

An icestorm in Canada and the USA in 1998 caused $650 million worth of damage.

The Great Storm of 1987 was the biggest to hit the UK during the 20th century.

A cluster of tornadoes in the USA in 1985 killed 271 and caused $400 million damage.

More than 45,000 people were trapped by avalanches in the Alps in January 1951.

Heat and dust

In hot countries, the Sun is the greatest killer. Drought occurs when the rains do not come. Without water, crops fail, animals die of thirst and people starve. Africa is prone to drought, most notably in the mid-1980s when millions in Ethiopia and Sudan starved. It took a major international aid program to stave off complete disaster. Severe drought in the Great Plains region of the USA in the 1930s turned vast stretches of farmland to dust, which simply blew away in the wind.

The Sahara Desert is growing by up to 100km every year – due in part to drought.

When the wind blows

'Hurricane', 'typhoon' and 'cyclone' are different names for the same force of nature. It is a circular, rotating storm that forms at sea and may be to up to 600km across. With winds reaching 300 km/h, it can devastate coastal regions. Cyclones are found in the Indian Ocean, typhoons occur in the western Pacific, while hurricanes rip though the Caribbean and the southern coasts of the USA. The winds and heavy rain sink ships, destroy houses and cause flooding. A hurricane that struck Texas, USA, in 1900 killed 8,000 people.

Hurricanes are usually given names, such as Juan, in 1985, Andrew, in 1992, and Floyd, in 1999.

FLOOD TIDE
A cyclone that hit Bangladesh in 1991 killed up to 200,000 people, mainly through floods caused by rain and high seas.

PLANTS

Plants are crucial for life. They provide most of the oxygen that animals and humans breathe – and much of the food they eat.

GIANTS
Redwoods are the largest trees in the world. One specimen measured 112.1m in height. These massive trees take 400 to 500 years to mature and live for up to 1,500 years.

RINGING THE CHANGES
Each year a tree produces a new layer or ring of wood. A dead tree's age can be calculated by counting the rings.

Plant

From tiny algae to massive trees, plants are everywhere. Some, such as roses, have colourful flowers, while others, like mosses, seem drab – yet each species suits its environment. Unlike animals, plants cannot move to find food and so must make their own using a process called photosynthesis. Plants contain a substance called chlorophyll – usually located in the leaves – which absorbs sunlight. This, mixed with minerals and water drawn from the soil by the roots, creates the energy plants need to grow.

Some plants rely on the wind to carry their pollen to another plant.

HOTLIPS PLANT
The bright, lipstick-red leaves of the hotlips plant are designed to attract insects to its tiny yellow flower.

Flowers

Plants evolved 550 million years ago, yet the first flowers only appeared 420 million years later. Plants that have flowers use them to reproduce. Bright flowers, such as cherry blossom, contain sugary nectar that attracts insects, especially bees. As a bee feeds, pollen from the male part of the flower is rubbed onto the insect's body. If the bee then feeds on another cherry blossom, some pollen is rubbed off onto the female part of the flower, fertilizing it so that it can produce seeds and fruit.

DEAD HORSE ARUM
This plant stinks of rotten meat to attract flies. They crawl inside to lay eggs and pick up pollen on the way.

Fungi

Fungi are not strictly plants or animals. They do not have leaves and roots and do not not make their own food. Instead, they feed on other animals and plants. Mushrooms are the visible fruiting parts of fungi. Most of a fungus' body consists of fine threads, which remain hidden underground or in the body of a dead tree or animal where they absorb nutrients. Although fungi such as field mushrooms, truffles and morels are good to eat, many species, such as the harmless-looking death cap, are deadly poisonous.

TOADSTOOL
Poisonous mushrooms, such as fly agaric, are often called toadstools. Fly agaric causes severe illness if eaten.

Predators

In areas of poor soil, some plants have evolved to get vital minerals from an unusual source – animals. These plants have special leaves or hairs that trap insects and even small frogs, which they then slowly digest. Pitcher plants attract insects using sweet scent. As a hungry insect climbs into the plant's slippery 'mouth', it loses its footing and is propelled by tiny hairs into a pool of digestive juices at the bottom. There is no escape!

Some plants, such as snowdrops and strangler figs, gain all their food by living on other plants.

DATABANK

INPUT

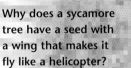

Q How much of the world's land surface is covered with rainforest?

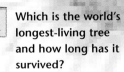

Q Why does a sycamore tree have a seed with a wing that makes it fly like a helicopter?

Q Which is the world's longest-living tree and how long has it survived?

OUTPUT

A About 7 per cent. However, it contains at least half of all animal species.

A The tree uses 'flying' seeds to help them reach ground suitable for growing.

A In California, USA, a bristlecone pine – called *Methuselah* – is 4,765 years old.

SWEET DRINK
Like insects, a few species of bats and birds feed on nectar and help to pollinate certain types of plant.

SNAP SHUT
If an insect lands in the open jaws of a Venus fly trap, it touches tiny hairs which set off the trap in an instant.

PREHISTORIC ANIMALS

Animals lived on Earth for hundreds of millions of years before the first humans appeared. Early creatures were tiny, but later huge beasts appeared – from earth-shaking dinosaurs to bizarre, ferocious mammals.

DIPLOCAULUS
Early amphibians were very strange looking. *Diplocaulus*, for example, had a boomerang-shaped head.

In the beginning

Life, in the form of bacteria and algae, first appeared in the oceans some 3,500 million years ago. However, the earliest fossils date from about 550 million years ago and consist of simple sponges, worms and trilobites. Now extinct, trilobites, which resembled large woodlice, were among the first animals to develop eyes. They were followed by creatures with shells, such as snails. Fish appeared about 500 million years ago. One species, *Dunkleosteus*, grew to 9m long – twice the size of a great white shark! By 400–300 million years ago, sea levels dropped and swamps became more common. Some fish developed legs, could breathe air, and were able to move about on land. These evolved into the first amphibians.

FOSSILS
Fossils, like this ammonite, form when animal bones or shells are covered with sediment layers. Over time, these remains are replaced by solid rock. Fossils can be preserved for millions of years.

The first land creatures were the arthropods – forerunners of the insects of today.

Dinosaurs

Amphibians were the earliest large land animals. However, they still relied heavily on water to survive and, with the rise of the reptiles, most became extinct. Reptiles evolved from amphibians but were better adapted to life on land. The largest and most successful reptiles were the dinosaurs, which means 'terrible lizards'. They ruled the Earth for 180 million years. Most dinosaurs were plant-eaters, and one of the largest of these was *Seismosaurus*, which was 50m long and weighed a titanic 90 tonnes. Like antelopes of today, many dinosaurs lived in huge herds. They were preyed upon by gigantic predators, such as *Allosaurus* and *Tyrannosaurus* – the lions of their time. All dinosaurs died out suddenly 65 million years ago.

Before the 1820s, dinosaur bones were thought to be those of dragons or even giant people.

HORNS OF A DILEMMA
Triceratops had huge horns on its head. These may have been used for defence against the terrifying *Tyrannosaurus rex*.

24

Up, up and away

As the dinosaurs ruled the land, other reptiles took to the air. Known as pterosaurs, these creatures' leathery wings consisted of skin held outstretched by elongated finger bones. Although most species were small, *Quetzalcoatlus* and *Pteranodon* were the largest flying animals that have ever lived. The oldest known bird is the fully feathered *Archaeopteryx*, which is thought to have evolved from a tiny dinosaur. Today, some zoologists regard birds as modern-day dinosaurs. Reptiles also conquered the oceans. Some of these were huge. *Kronosaurus*, for example, had a skull 2.7m long – larger and more powerful than that of *Tyrannosaurus rex*! Other carnivorous sea reptiles, called ichthyosaurs – 'fish lizards' – resembled a cross between a shark and a dolphin.

FLYING NIGHTMARE
Quetzalcoatlus is the largest flying reptile found so far. Its 12m wingspan is equivalent to that of a small plane or glider.

Elasmosaurus, a sea reptile, had a flexible neck 8m long. It was expert at catching fish.

EARLY BIRD
Archaeopteryx was probably not a strong flier. It may have had to climb trees to gain enough height to fly or glide.

 Early mammals

Mammals existed as early as 200 million years ago, but they remained small until the dinosaurs became extinct. After this time, however, many mammals evolved to become as big as the reptiles they replaced. *Indricotherium*, a relative of the rhino, was 8m long and weighed 30 tonnes – twice the size of the woolly mammoth, which was a giant ancestor of the modern elephant.

EARLY SHREW
Early mammals resembled shrews. They foraged only at night when the dinosaurs were inactive.

DATABANK

Q Why did the dinosaurs become extinct?

A Many scientists believe that the dinosaurs died out after a huge meteorite struck Earth.

Q Which animals did mammals evolve from?

A Mammals may have evolved from a group of mammal-like reptiles called cynodonts.

SMILER
The size of a lion, *Smilodon* may have preyed on animals as large as elephants. The elongated canine teeth might have been used to stab its victims to death.

FACTS AND FIGURES

A flightless bird, *Diatryma*, was large enough to catch horses in its massive beak.

The first dinosaur to be discovered was *Megalosaurus* – named in the 1820s.

It is thought that 99.9 per cent of all species that have ever existed are now extinct.

Tyrannosaurus' teeth were 15cm long, about the size of a banana – but sharper!

The smallest known dinosaur was *Compsognathus*. It was about the size of a chicken.

INVERTEBRATES

Unlike fish, reptiles and mammals, invertebrates have no backbone. From tiny mites to giant squid, they include some of the world's most amazing animals.

SOCIAL WORK
Leaf-cutter ants collect leaves for food for their colony. Each ant brings back a load heavier than itself.

AIR HOLES
As earthworms tunnel, they let oxygen into the soil. In areas that lack worms, soil quality is very poor.

Alien lifeforms

Invertebrates often appear alien to us and so we fear them. For example, jellyfish have no eyes, while crabs, sponges and worms lack recognizable heads. Yet some invertebrates are highly intelligent. Octopuses can unscrew jar lids to get at food and also quickly learn new skills by watching others. The robber crab, a species that lives almost entirely on land, climbs palm trees to cut down coconuts. It then returns to the ground to feed.

THE STING
Jellyfish have soft bodies and tentacles armed with venomous stings. These are used to paralyze their prey.

The Great Barrier Reef in Australia is the largest structure made by animals – built by billions of tiny corals.

Insects

Insects are the most common animals on Earth, with about a million species, including butterflies, beetles, flies, wasps and grasshoppers. Insects do not have internal skeletons like humans, but instead have a hard exterior, like a suit of armour. Some insects, such as bees and ants, work together to find food and fight off enemies. Millions of ants may live together in one nest serving a single queen. The queen ant's only job is to lay eggs.

BIG BEETLE
The heaviest insect is the goliath beetle. It grows as big as a man's fist and weighs up to 100g.

FACTS AND FIGURES

The goliath bird-eating spider is the world's largest. Spread out, its legs span up to 28cm.

It is thought there may be 10 million species of insects still to be discovered.

A giant clam discovered off Japan's coast weighed 340kg – the largest shellfish ever.

Tropical cockroaches run at speeds equivalent to a human sprinting at 330 km/h.

The caterpillar of a *Polythemus* moth eats 86,000 times its birthweight before pupating.

ATLAS MOTH
With a 25–30cm wingspan, this moth is often mistaken for a bird. It has the largest antennae of any moth.

WOODY DISGUISE
Stick insects closely resemble the twigs they live on. One species is the longest of all insects, measuring over 50cm.

Arachnids

Scorpions and spiders are arachnids, and not insects. They are among the world's most feared animals. In some cases, fear is justified. One species of Mexican scorpion kills more than 1,000 people a year, and it is claimed that the black widow spider's venom is 15 times more powerful than that of a rattlesnake. Many spiders spin a sticky web in order to catch food. The largest webs, at 1.5m in diameter, are those of the orb-weaving spider, which can catch small birds. Spider silk is the strongest of all natural or man-made fibres. Scientists are trying to recreate it in laboratories so that it can be used by humans.

TAIL OF WOE
A scorpion has a sting in the end of its tail. This is mainly used in self-defence against animals that try to eat it.

Fishermen of Papua New Guinea use the huge webs of orb-weaving spiders as fishing nets.

Giants of the deep

For centuries, stories of giant sea monsters were dismissed as myths. In 1887, however, the body of a giant squid was washed ashore on Cook Strait, New Zealand. It measured 18.9m from the tip of its tail to the end of its tentacles. Since then, more bodies have been found, but few people have ever seen a live specimen. The world's largest invertebrates, giant squid remain a great mystery to science as they glide through the ocean depths.

Giant squid are molluscs and so are related to octopuses, giant clams and even garden snails!

TITANS
Whalers have caught sperm whales that had strange disc-like wounds. Experts believe these were made by a giant squid's huge suckers as the whale tried to make a meal of the squid.

DATABANK

INPUT

Q What animals are known as crustaceans and which is the largest in the world?

Q Is a starfish a species of fish or is it an invertebrate?

Q Which is the most dangerous invertebrate to humans?

OUTPUT

A Crustaceans include crabs, lobsters and prawns. The largest is the spider crab.

A It is an invertebrate. Starfish are closely related to sea urchins and sea cucumbers.

A The mosquito. It spreads diseases such as malaria which kill thousands every year.

FINS AND SCALES

Fish, amphibians and reptiles were the first vertebrates – animals with backbones. While fish live in water, reptiles survive happily on land. Amphibians live between the two.

 ## Fish

Fish differ from other vertebrates because they have gills, which allow them to breathe underwater. There are 24,000 species of fish, of which 60 per cent live in the sea. They range in size from a species of goby barely the length of a thumbnail to the 12m-long whale shark. Despite its name, the whale shark feeds on tiny fish and plankton and is not dangerous. Not all fish are tied to water. Flying fish leap out of the sea to escape danger and glide up to 400m on stiff fins that act as wings. The African lungfish can survive for up to four years encased in mud if the pond it lives in dries up. It can even breathe air using a primitive type of lung. When the rains come, it crawls out of its sanctuary and looks for food.

Archerfish fire water at insects on overhanging leaves to shoot them down. The insects are then eaten.

FISH FATHERHOOD
A female seahorse lays eggs in a pouch on the male's body. He protects the young until they can fend for themselves.

DATABANK

Q How does an electric eel produce electricity and what does it use it for?

A The eel produces and stores electricity in special muscles. It uses this power to stun prey.

Q Which is the longest snake in the world and what sort of food does it eat?

A The reticulated python reaches up to 10m in length. Its normal diet includes small mammals.

POND PARENTS
A male stickleback (red) makes a nest and entices a female to lay her eggs inside it. He then cares for the eggs and young.

FISH VOYAGE
Born in the Sargasso Sea, European eels migrate to European rivers where they live until adulthood. They return to the Sargasso to breed. Eels can move across land to new waters.

GREAT WHITE TRAGEDY
Feared because of films like *Jaws*, the great white shark is heavily hunted. Today, there may be fewer than 5,000 left.

North America

Europe

Africa

South America

Sargasso Sea

Atlantic Ocean

Reptiles

In the past there were many different types of reptile, but today there are only snakes, lizards, turtles and crocodiles. A typical reptile has dry, scaly skin and lays eggs. Many lizards have a surprising defence mechanism. If one is caught by a predator, it sheds its tail so that it can escape. Later, it grows another tail. One species that has no such worries is the Komodo dragon. Reaching 3m long, it hunts animals as large as water buffalo – and humans!

An estimated one million people are bitten by snakes every year – up to 40,000 of whom die.

FULL THROTTLE
Boa constrictors kill prey, such as this coypu, by suffocation. As the animal tries to breathe, the snake squeezes tighter.

FACTS AND FIGURES

A giant tortoise lived from 1766 to 1918. It had survived for at least 152 years!

The sailfish swims at speeds in excess of 100 km/h – the fastest fish in the seas.

The largest frog of all is the goliath frog. At 3.5kg, it is the size of a chicken!

There are over 4,200 species of amphibian and about 6,800 species of reptile.

Amphibians

While reptiles have tough skin, amphibians, such as frogs, toads and salamanders, have thin, moist skin and must stay near water to avoid drying out. Most must also lay their eggs in water. At first, a young frog or toad is called a tadpole. It resembles a small fish and cannot survive on land. Over time, however, the tadpole's long tail shrinks and it develops legs and lungs. By the time it looks like its parents, it can breathe air and spends increasingly long periods out of water.

The world's largest amphibian is the giant salamander which reaches 1.8m long and 65kg.

A paradoxical frog tadpole reaches 16cm in length but turns into an adult frog only 5–6cm long!

DEADLY FROG
Poison-dart frogs carry deadly toxins. A golden poison-dart frog has enough poison to kill 1,000 people.

BIRDS

Birds are not only masters of the air but have conquered nearly every other habitat. They can be found roosting in mountain ranges, diving for fish in the ice cold seas of the Antarctic or nesting in the bleakest deserts.

Flying

Birds have three features that set them apart from other animals – feathers, hollow bones and bills. Feathers make sturdy wings for flight, and protect against heat and cold. Their bones are hollow so they are light enough for flight, and the bills of different species are adapted to feed on all kinds of food, such as seeds or meat. Birds have different flight methods. Hummingbirds hover on wings that beat up to 90 times a second. Albatrosses, by contrast, glide without flapping their wings. The Arctic tern uses this energy-saving method to make the annual round trip of 16,000km from its breeding territory in the Arctic to winter feeding grounds in the Antarctic – and back again. In a lifetime, this is equal to flying to the Moon and back!

A pet male budgerigar called Puck, from California, USA, had a vocabulary of 1,728 human words.

SWEET FEAST
Hummingbirds have very long tongues and bills in order to reach the sugary nectar deep inside tropical flowers.

BIG BILL
The toucan's huge bill is up to half the length of its body. The bill has internal struts to make it both strong and light. The bright colouring is vital for attracting mates in the breeding season.

FACTS AND FIGURES

The prehistoric *Teratornis* was the biggest flying bird ever. It had a 6m wingspan.

The smallest bird is the bee hummingbird. It is 57mm long, including bill and tail.

The fastest flier is the peregrine falcon, which can dive at over 250 km/h.

Birds such as geese and swans can fly at over 9,000m – higher than Mt Everest.

North American passenger pigeons, now extinct, lived in flocks of over 2,000 million.

The red-billed quelea is the most numerous bird today, with over 1,500 million adults.

There are between 8,500 and 10,000 bird species in the world.

DATABANK

INPUT		OUTPUT	
Q	Why do birds such as swallows migrate each year?	**A**	Birds migrate long distances looking for fresh sources of food.
Q	Which is the largest bird of prey and what does it eat?	**A**	The Andean condor, which feeds on dead animals, reaches 12kg.
Q	Which is the rarest bird and how many are left in the wild?	**A**	In 1999, only one Spix's macaw was living in the wild.
Q	Which is the world's most dangerous bird to humans?	**A**	The cassowary, of Australia. It is 2m tall and can kill a human.

Grounded

Some birds have lost the ability to fly. The ostrich, the world's largest bird, uses its muscular legs to run at up to 70 km/h in order to escape danger. Yet giving up flying can be risky. The dodo, from the island of Mauritius, had no enemies until sailors arrived and hunted it for food. It became extinct in 1662. The rare kakapo of New Zealand is a flightless parrot. It is endangered because its nests, which it builds on the ground, are raided by rats.

EGG-STREME
The ostrich lays an egg weighing up to 2kg – big enough to make 12 standard omelettes.

Some birds rarely come to ground. Sooty terns remain airborne for up to 10 years and only land to breed.

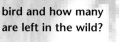

Chick and egg

Egg-laying and nests are not unique to birds, but birds produce the widest variety. The mute swan lays one of the biggest eggs, 12cm long, of any flying bird. It needs a nest 1.5m wide to hold its clutch. In contrast, the vervain hummingbird lays a 10mm egg – a fraction of the size. While many newly hatched chicks are helpless and take weeks to develop, the young malleefowl of southern Australia flies by the time it is only 24 hours old.

HELPLESS YOUNGSTER
It takes a chick hours to break out of its shell. Most baby birds depend on their parents for food for weeks after.

FOSTER-CHICK
Cuckoos lay eggs in the nests of smaller birds. When it hatches, the chick is fed by the parents as if it were their own.

Birds of prey

Birds of prey, such as eagles, are very efficient hunters. They have powerful claws in order to kill and carry off prey, and sharp bills with which to eat it. Eagles soar high above the land, using eyesight several times keener than ours to locate food. The peregrine falcon, which catches other birds in mid-air, can spot its prey up to a remarkable 8km away.

CLEAN UP
Vultures feed on the carcasses of dead animals. By cleaning up, they prevent diseases from spreading.

A nest belonging to a pair of bald eagles, Florida, USA, was found to weigh almost three tonnes.

MAMMALS

There are over 4,000 species of mammals, in every shape and size. They are found all over the world, and have mastered the sea and air as well as the land.

Mammal world

The world's smallest mammal is Kitti's hog-nosed bat from Thailand, which weighs 2g – less than a table-tennis ball. It would take 75 million of these bumblebee-sized bats to equal the weight of the world's largest mammal, the blue whale. On land, African elephants are the heavyweight champions, but the largest hunters are polar bears. With their thick coats of fur, they endure temperatures as low as –40°C, travelling up to 1,200km a year across the ice in search of food. By contrast, the addax, a small antelope, braves the heat of the Sahara Desert where the midday temperature can reach a fierce 50°C. It survives by taking all of its water from the vegetation it eats. Both the addax and polar bear live in small groups, but some mammals gather in vast herds. In eastern Africa, about 2 million wildebeest and 300,000 plains zebras migrate thousands of kilometres between feeding-grounds each year, following the seasonal rain. Yet today, many mammal species are becoming rare. There are as few as 700 giant pandas left in China due to the destruction of their forest home.

A female true lemming can become pregnant at the age of just 14 days and give birth 16 days later.

LAND GIANT
The biggest African elephant weighed about 12 tonnes – much more than a double decker bus full of passengers.

There are an estimated 5.3 billion rats in the world – almost 1 rat for every human being.

HUNTED HUNTER
At 2.8m long, the tiger is the largest cat. It has been heavily hunted and less than 5,000 now survive in the wild.

FACTS AND FIGURES

The rarest large mammal is the Javan rhinoceros. There are less than 70 in the wild.

At 6m tall, the giraffe can peer through the window of a third-floor apartment.

The koala is one of the sleepiest mammals. It spends 22 hours of the day dozing.

The fastest mammal is the cheetah. This hunting cat reaches 100 km/h.

The fin whale may live to be 90 years old, making it the longest lived wild mammal.

Strange but true

Some mammals have bizarre appearances. Bats have developed wings that enable them to fly like birds. The largest bats are called flying foxes, and some species have a wingspan of 2m. The Mexican free-tailed bat lives in colonies containing 50 million individuals. There are so many bats that over 100,000 tonnes of droppings have been dug out of a single bat cave to be used as fertilizer.

A truly weird mammal is the duck-billed platypus. It looks like a furry otter but has a huge, duck-like beak and webbed feet that end in sharp claws. Strangest of all, a female platypus lays eggs, which she then sits on until they hatch.

A giant anteater eats 30,000 ants and termites in a day, which it catches with its long, sticky tongue.

FRUIT BATTY
A quarter of all mammal species are bats. Some eat insects, while others, like this one, feed on fruit.

GORILLA
Male mountain gorillas weigh about 165kg and have an arm span of 2.75m – big enough to hug four people.

Just like us

Humans belong to a group of mammals known as primates, which also contains monkeys, chimpanzees and gorillas. Chimps share an incredible 98 per cent of human genes and have a well-developed brain. They live in complex family groups, and hunt and play together. Some individuals have even learned to use sticks and rocks as tools, such as chisels and hammers. The smallest primates are mouse lemurs, which are just 6cm long, with a 13cm tail.

Dolphins are small whales. The largest species of dolphin is the killer whale or orca.

 Sea monsters

Whales are the largest animals on Earth, yet despite their size they can swim swiftly. Blue whales reach speeds of 48 km/h if alarmed. The sperm whale, which weighs 70 tonnes, is the world's biggest predator. It dives to record depths of 3,000m hunting fish. Walruses and seals are also at home at sea. The crab-eater seal is the most common large sea mammal, with a population of 30 million in Antarctica.

BIGGEST IN THE WORLD
The longest blue whale ever caught was measured at 33.58m from tip to tail. The heaviest whale weighed 190 tonnes.

INTO THE PAST

In ancient and medieval times, great civilizations rose and fell. Some lasted for hundreds of years and left a deep impression on history by shaping today's laws, customs and even political boundaries.

CEREMONY
Ancient Egypt's supreme god was Amon. His throned statue was lavished with gifts during religious rites.

Egyptians

Egypt was one of the world's first great civilizations. It rose 5,000 years ago and lasted for 3,000 years until it was absorbed into the Roman Empire. The river Nile regularly flooded, producing fertile land that gave the Egyptians the wealth to build grand monuments and establish a highly sophisticated society. Egyptians invented hieroglyphics, a form of writing based on pictures, and also developed the calendar.

In Egypt, the king was treated as a god and had total power over his many subjects.

MUMMY
An Egyptian king's body was soaked in spices and wrapped in linen bandages to preserve it for the afterlife.

Classical times

Ancient Greece was made up of independent city states, such as Thebes, Sparta and Athens, that came to prominence in 500–150BC. Greek culture inspired enlightened thinkers, such as Aristotle and Plato, and writers like Euripides and Sophocles. The work of such men still influences modern politics, literature, art and science. Like Egypt, Greece was eventually conquered by the Romans. The Romans were principally soldiers and administrators but their culture was based on Greek ideas, which they allowed to spread throughout their massive empire.

ROME'S RISE
At its height, the Roman Empire extended from Britain to Egypt and from Spain to the Caspian Sea in Asia.

Londinium (London)
Lutetia (Paris)
Asia
Caspian Sea
Europe
Rome
Athens
Carthage
Jerusalem
Alexandria
Africa

FACTS AND FIGURES

The Chinese first used explosives in battle in 1161 at the battle of Ts'ai-shih.

Rome, with a population of 1 million in AD100, was the largest city of its age.

The oldest evidence for the domestication of animals comes from Iraq in 8650BC.

England's Henry V, with 6,000 men, beat a French army of 25,000 at Agincourt, in 1415.

ENLIGHTENED
Greek culture was able to flourish without outside threat after the Greek states, led by Athens, defeated the invading Persians at Marathon in 490BC and Salamis in 480BC.

DATABANK

 Q Which is the oldest town in the world, and how many people used to live there?

 A Jericho dates from at least 9000BC. By 8000BC, it held 2,000 people. The site is still inhabited.

 Q Is it true that part of the Roman Empire survived the fall of Rome itself?

A The Eastern Empire lasted until 1453. Constantinople (now Istanbul, Turkey) was its capital.

Middle Ages

The fall of the Roman Empire in about AD500 was followed by the conquest of the Mediterranean 200 years later by Arab followers of Islam. While Europe entered the Dark Ages – a period of disorder – areas under Arab control, particularly Spain, saw a great revival of learning. The Arab army, numbering 80,000, was finally halted at the Battle of Tours in AD732 by the 40,000 strong forces of the Frankish king Charles Martel. The Christian kings of Europe, led by the Pope, fought back with the 'reconquest' of Spain, and launched crusades to 'free' the Holy Land. In the Far East, war and invasion were also common. The Chinese empire, another area of great learning, was conquered by the nomadic Mongols in 1234. These warriors overran Asia and even threatened Europe. They reached Vienna in 1241, before turning back after the death of their leader, Ogedei Khan.

HIGH SOCIETY
Mayans evolved a sophisticated civilization in the mountains of Central and South America, in AD250–1650.

LANCE A LOT
Tournaments were the sports championships of the Middle Ages and helped knights practise key battle skills.

Of the nine crusades to the Holy Land only the first (1096–99) succeeded in its aim of capturing Jerusalem.

JOUSTING
Charging knights used lances to unseat their opponents. A knight was declared to be the loser once he fell off his horse.

HISTORICAL FIGURES

History is filled with colourful characters. Some were great warriors or fierce tyrants who stamped their mark on history, others are remembered for their inspirational deeds and words.

Ancient thinkers

Greeks like Aristotle, Archimedes and Plato, and the Islamic philosopher Averroës have shaped much of western scientific and philosophical thought. Aristotle is one of history's great all-rounders – he was expert in logic, ethics, politics, psychology, physics, biology *and* poetry! In the East, the Chinese philosopher Confucius (551–479BC) developed a system of thought that remained the state religion of China until recently.

CONFUCIUS
The name Confucius is Latin for K'ung Fu-Tzu. He was a Chinese minister who became a wandering sage.

Defenders

The most popular leaders have been those who defend their people, often against great odds or against injustice. In Egypt about 3,500 years ago, the Hebrew people were subject to the tyrannic rule of the pharaohs – until Moses came to lead them. According to legend, Moses parted the Red Sea to enable his people to escape. He led the Hebrews through many hardships before they reached the promised land of Israel. Boudicca, Queen of the Iceni tribe in ancient Britain, valiantly led her people against Roman occupation in the 1st century AD. After several victories, including the burning of Roman London, her forces were crushed. Boudicca drank poison rather than be captured.

Archimedes was killed when, immersed in a maths problem, he ignored an attacking Roman soldier.

As well as being a great resistance fighter, King Alfred encouraged learning and promoted justice.

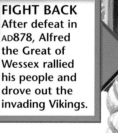

FIGHT BACK
After defeat in AD878, Alfred the Great of Wessex rallied his people and drove out the invading Vikings.

MARTYR
In 1429, Joan of Arc led the French to victory against the English who were besieging Orléans. She was later betrayed and was burned for 'sorcery'. She was made a saint in 1920.

CIVIL WARRIOR
One of Abraham Lincoln's reasons for fighting the South in the US Civil War (1861–65) was to abolish slavery.

MIGHTY EMPIRE
Genghis Khan's field army was cavalry. This meant he could launch swift surprise attacks, decimating armies of foot soldiers.

Conquerors

In the past, conquest and victory in battle was a way of gaining wealth and uniting a people. A successful conqueror was popular. One of the most feared was the Mongol Genghis Khan (1162–1227). He rose from obscurity to unify the semi-barbaric tribes of Mongolia, massacring his enemies. When he defeated the Tartars, he killed everyone 'above the height of a cart axle'. The Mongols went on to conquer China at a cost of millions of lives. Another formidable general, Napoleon Bonaparte (1769–1821) led France's armies to victory at Austerlitz (1805) and Jena (1806). For a few years, he held all of Europe save Britain. He was eventually captured at the Battle of Waterloo (1815) and exiled to the island of St Helena in the Atlantic Ocean.

Ivan IV of Russia (1530–84) was known as Ivan the Terrible due to his strong rule and victories in war.

LEGENDARY
One of the greatest generals the world has ever seen, Alexander the Great conquered an empire from Greece to India by 326BC – a feat a modern army would find hard to match.

FACTS AND FIGURES

William I (the Conqueror) defeated Harold II at Hastings to become king of England.

English king Henry VIII had six different wives during his 38-year reign.

Constantine the Great became the first Christian Emperor of the Roman Empire in AD312.

In 1871 'Iron' Chancellor Otto Von Bismarck united Germany into a single country.

George Washington became the first President of the USA in 1789.

FAIR QUEEN
Elizabeth I's English fleet defeated the Spanish Armada in 1585, and so kept England independent.

SNOW WAY FORWARD
Napoleon invaded Russia in 1812 but was forced back by terrible weather. Much of his powerful army froze to death.

EXPLORERS

Throughout history, adventurers have risked their lives crossing strange countries and seas in search of new lands, fame and fortune. For many, however, death was their only reward.

Australia

The first explorers to reach Australia may have been the Chinese in the 15th century. In the 16th century, Portuguese and Spanish explorers claimed to have discovered *terra australis incognita* – the 'unknown southern land'. By 1642 Dutch navigators, particularly Abel Tasman, had mapped Australia's western coast, Tasmania and New Zealand. However, it was Captain James Cook who charted Australia's eastern coast and claimed the new lands for England in 1770. Cook made several more voyages in the Pacific and even ventured as far south as Antarctica.

The first settlers of Australia were the Aboriginal people who arrived from Asia some 40,000 years ago.

In 1912, Captain Robert Scott's expedition to the South Pole perished in the icy wastes.

Marco Polo

In the early Middle Ages, Europeans knew little about China and the Far East except through travellers' tales brought back by traders. In 1271, however, the Venetian merchant, Marco Polo, set off with his father and uncle on an epic expedition that was to open people's eyes. After crossing Turkey, Iran, Afghanistan, India and most of China, the Polos spent 17 years as guests of the Mongol Emperor Kublai Khan, visiting places never before seen by Europeans. Marco wrote down his experiences when he returned home. Although many people did not believe him, merchants were encouraged to travel east and seek their fortunes.

GOOD COOK
James Cook ensured that his ship's crew ate a balanced diet and so did not succumb to diseases like scurvy. Cook himself was killed by natives on the island of Hawaii in 1779.

FACTS AND FIGURES

In 1953, Edmund Hillary and Norgay Tenzing became the first men to climb Mt Everest.

The first journey to the South Pole was made in 1911 by Roald Amundsen of Norway.

Vasco da Gama of Portugal sailed around the Cape of Good Hope to India in 1497.

Juan Sebastien del Cano of Spain was the first to sail around the world, 1519–22.

In 1909, American Robert Peary became the first man to reach the North Pole.

Amerigo Vespucci, from Italy, explored the coast of South America 1499–1501.

SEASONED TRAVELLERS
Even after they had reached China, the Polos spent many years exploring the vast provinces of the Mongol Empire.

Venice
China
Iran
India

GO EAST
It took the Polos four years to reach China. They had to cross several mountain ranges and endure dry, inhospitable deserts filled with wild animals and armed bandits.

The New World

Exactly which European first discovered the Americas is the subject of great debate. Viking sagas tell of Leif Ericsson who landed on the North American continent in AD1000 at a place he named 'Vinland' because of the wild grapes he found growing there. Remains of a Viking settlement have been discovered in Newfoundland, Canada. However, the man most commonly credited with discovering both North and South America is Christopher Columbus. Born in Genoa, Italy, Columbus believed that he could find a short cut to Asia by sailing west across the Atlantic Ocean.

Early explorers of the Americas believed they had landed in Asia and so called the native people 'Indians'.

UNSETTLED
A Viking named Thorfinn tried to establish a permanent colony in 'Vinland'. He had to abandon his plans three years later due to hostility from the native North Americans.

LAND AHOY!
Columbus (red) sailed across the Atlantic to the Carribean. The Vikings (blue) stayed closer to the coasts. They only found America when a storm blew one of their ships far off course.

Greenland
Norway
Vinland
Spain
Caribbean
Atlantic Ocean

Columbus had difficulty gaining support for his expedition, but he finally set sail in August 1492. After a perilous voyage, he reached what was probably the Bahamas in October. He then visited Cuba and Haiti before heading home. On later voyages, Columbus reached the Gulf of Mexico and South America. However, it was John Cabot, also from Genoa, who discovered the North American mainland in 1497.

SMALL SQUADRON
Columbus's ships were called the *Santa Maria*, *Niña* and *Pinta*. Their combined crews totalled only 120 men.

REVOLUTION AND WAR

Revolutions change the social, political and economic structure of a country. But the most far-reaching changes are brought about by war, which can devastate entire regions and populations.

BRITS OUT
The American colonies revolted against British rule in 1775 because of oppressively high taxes.

Revolutions

Revolutions occur when a country's people are suffering hardship. If people believe their rulers are the cause of their suffering or are not prepared to help, their anger may become a violent uprising. Reprisals can be severe. The peasant revolts in England in 1381 and Germany in 1525 were put down with great brutality by the landowners.

After a major war with Britain, the American colonies won independence with the Treaty of Paris in 1783.

RUSSIAN REVOLUTION
In October 1917, Russian communists seized the Winter Palace in St Petersburg, sweeping away the old corrupt monarchy.

FACTS AND FIGURES

Simón Bolívar (1783–1830) led revolts in Venezuela, Columbia, Ecuador and Peru.

In 1282, Sicilians massacred their French rulers in what is known as the Sicilian Vespers.

Many modern ideas of freedom and democracy stem from the French Revolution.

Up to 65 million soldiers were mobilized in World War I. 8.5 million were killed.

The Vietnam War (1955–75) claimed the lives of over 2 million Vietnamese people.

The Iran-Iraq War of 1980–88 cost each side 500,000 casualties with little gain.

Tanks were used for the first time in 1916. They made it easier to attack in battle.

Off with her head...

In 1789, France was ruled by a corrupt government and king, Louis XVI, who spent vast sums on luxuries. Meanwhile, people starved as harvests failed and food prices rose. They demanded justice. Riots broke out in many areas, members of the ruling class were murdered and the king was arrested in 1792 to be executed a year later. The old political system was replaced by the Republic, which aimed at 'liberty, equality and fraternity' for all. However, it was followed by the Reign of Terror – a ten-month period of execution and murder – until a moderate government took control.

THE TERROR
Up to 20,000 'enemies of the Revolution' were beheaded on the guillotine during the Reign of Terror.

Conflict

War is conflict between the armies of two nations or states or between groups within a state (known as civil war). Wars start for many reasons. A country may attack another to gain land, wealth or even revenge. Wars are violent and many die. The United Nations was set up in 1945 to try to prevent wars.

MASS DESTRUCTION
War in the 20th century has seen the development of deadly weapons, such as Germany's *V2* rocket in World War II.

CIVIL WAR
The American Civil War, (1861–65) was fought between two groups of states, the Union and Confederates.

TRENCHES
In World War I, soldiers dug trenches for protection from enemy fire. Trenches were hard to attack.

HOPE TURNS TO SLAUGHTER
Soldiers went to war in 1914 in high spirits. By September 1918, millions of them had died in grim trench warfare.

World War I

World War I (1914–18) was caused by distrust between the major powers. The Allies – France, Russia and the British Empire, with later help from Italy and the USA, fought against Germany, Austria-Hungary and Turkey. After great carnage, the Allies prevailed, but at a terrible cost. Furthermore, the peace treaty made in 1919 helped cause World War II.

World War II

In 1939, the German army invaded Poland as part of the Nazis' plan to create a German Empire. This act forced the UK and France to declare war on Germany. The Nazis, allied with Italy and later Japan, went on to conquer most of Europe. The tide began to turn in 1941 with the USA's entry into the war and in 1942 with Russia's victory over the Germans at Stalingrad. However, victory was not achieved until 1945.

World War II led to the Cold War – a long period of tension between Russia and the USA.

FLATTENED IN AN INSTANT
Japan fought until August 1945 when the USA dropped atom bombs on Hiroshima and Nagasaki, killing 200,000 people.

20TH-CENTURY LEADERS

Some of the most famous and important people of the last century were our leaders. They took us into world wars, brought us peace, and still hold enormous influence over our everyday lives.

Politicians

An inspirational figure, British prime minister Winston Churchill led the fight against Germany, Italy and Japan during World War II (1939–45). A formidable tactician, Churchill was also a great public speaker and his stirring speeches encouraged people in Nazi-occupied Europe to resist Hitler. John F. Kennedy is probably the world's most famous peacetime leader. Elected in 1960 – one of the youngest US presidents – he is best remembered for supporting civil rights. After bringing the world to the brink of nuclear war during the Cuban missile crisis of 1962, he improved relations between Russia and the US, achieving a nuclear test ban.

The embalmed body of Russian revolutionary leader Lenin was displayed in public for many years.

MISSILE CRISIS
This cartoon depicts Russian leader Krushchev and US president Kennedy, close to nuclear war, in 1962.

WORLD WAR II ALLIES
Churchill, US president F. D. Roosevelt and Joseph Stalin, leader of Russia, met at Yalta in the Crimea, in 1945.

FACTS AND FIGURES

The first ever female prime minister was Sri Lanka's Sirimavo Bandaranaike, 1960.

It is claimed that there have been 600 attempts to kill Cuban leader Fidel Castro.

Pedro Lascurain was president of Mexico for one hour in 1913 before resigning.

Margaret Thatcher became the first woman prime minister of Britain in 1979.

Tibet's leader, the Dalai Lama, has been in exile since China invaded Tibet in 1950.

F. D. Roosevelt held power for 12 years – the longest serving US president.

Freedom fighters

The 20th century saw many crusaders for human rights. In India, Gandhi used non-violent protest to win independence for India from the British Empire in 1948. Nelson Mandela, head of the African National Congress, fought against South Africa's racist apartheid policy. Imprisoned by the government in 1964, he was finally released in 1990, and a year later apartheid was abolished. With South African president F. W. de Clerk, Mandela won the Nobel Peace Prize in 1993, and in 1994 he became South Africa's first black president.

GREAT SOUL
Famed all over the world for his peaceful protest, Gandhi is also known as the Mahatma, or 'great soul'.

'I HAVE A DREAM'
Influenced by Gandhi, Dr Martin Luther King Jr became a figurehead for black civil rights in America in the 1960s.

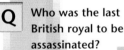

FASCIST SIDEKICK
Benito Mussolini became dictator of Italy in 1922. He was an ally of Hitler in World War II and was killed in 1945.

Hitler and other top Nazis committed suicide to avoid capture by their enemies.

Dictators

Dictators are leaders with unlimited power. Adolf Hitler of Germany was the most infamous dictator of all time. His attempts to create a vast empire in Europe led to World War II. The conflict caused worldwide suffering and up to 50 million people died. He was finally defeated in 1945 by the allies led by the USA, Britain and Russia. Russia's leader, Joseph Stalin, was also a powerful dictator. Stalin rose to power in 1922 and ordered many bloody purges to secure his leadership. Although responsible for over ten million deaths during his long rule, he was not overthrown, and died in power in 1953.

DATABANK

INPUT	OUTPUT
Q Does France have a king or queen?	**A** No. France has an elected president as the head of state.
Q Who was General Francisco Franco and where did he rule?	**A** An ally of Hitler, Franco was dictator of Spain from 1939–75.
Q Who was the last British royal to be assassinated?	**A** Lord Mountbatten was killed by Irish terrorists in 1979.
Q What was Ronald Reagan before he became US president?	**A** Reagan was originally an actor. He starred in 50 films.

HOLOCAUST
Hitler murdered millions of innocent people, including over six million Jews in concentration camps in Europe.

Russia and its empire used to be known as the USSR – the Union of Soviet Socialist Republics.

Assassination

Many leaders have been murdered for political or religious motives. Human rights leaders Gandhi and Martin Luther King were both killed by extremists angered by their work. In India in the 1980s, Gandhi's namesake, Rajiv, succeeded his mother Indira as prime minister after her assassination in 1984. However, he too was murdered by political enemies in 1991.

ARCHDUKE FRANZ FERDINAND
Ferdinand, heir to the throne of Austria, was assassinated in 1914 by Gavrilo Princip, a Slav nationalist. His death sparked off World War I.

THE ROMANOVS
Czar Nicholas II of Russia was forced to give up his throne after the 1917 revolution. A short time later, he and his entire family were shot.

PRESIDENT JOHN F. KENNEDY
Perhaps the most famous president of the USA, John F. Kennedy was assassinated in Dallas in 1963 by Lee Harvey Oswald.

INSIDE THE BODY

The body is a well-oiled machine. It appears smooth on the surface, but beneath the skin, muscles flex, the lungs inflate, the heart pumps and blood rushes to all parts of the body in order to keep us alive.

PUSH AND PULL
Muscles make up about half of the body's weight. If a muscle becomes damaged, it can repair itself.

SOFT CENTRE
Bones have a spongy core. This contains red bone marrow, a soft tissue that produces blood cells.

A human body is made up of 50 million million million cells. There are 100,000 genes in each cell.

FACTS AND FIGURES

The heart beats over two billion times in a lifetime without stopping.

The digestive system, from the mouth to the anus, is about 9m long.

The brain usually weighs about 1.4kg, but the heaviest recorded brain was 2.3kg.

A baby's heartbeat reaches 130 beats a minute – twice the rate of an adult heart.

The brain needs roughly its own weight in blood every minute to function.

Every day we breathe in and out about 25,000 times – over 17 times a minute.

Muscles

There are over 640 muscles in the body and they provide the forces that enable us to move. Merely walking requires the use of 200 of them. Constructed of strong, flexible fibres, muscles are attached to bones by cords called tendons. The largest tendon in the body is the Achilles, which connects the calf muscle to the heel bone. A muscle works by contracting – getting shorter – and pulling the bone it is attached to. After contracting, the muscle cannot straighten itself and has to be pulled back by another muscle. Therefore, muscles often work in pairs to move a bone backwards and forwards.

Much of a baby's skeleton is flexible cartilage. As the child grows, bone replaces the cartilage.

Skeleton

Like iron girders in a building, bones are the frames for our bodies. Without them we would collapse into a heap. Although they look dead, bones are living structures with blood vessels and nerves. There are 206 bones in the body and they come in all shapes and sizes. The longest and toughest is the thigh bone, which is about five times the strength of steel. The smallest is the stirrup bone in the ear, which aids hearing. It is only 3mm long.

SKULL
There are 22 bones in the skull. Eight bones protect the brain, while 14 make up the face.

HANDY WORK
Our hands and forearms contain over 30 muscles. These enable us to perform many intricate tasks with our fingers.

THE HEART OF THE MATTER
About the size of a grapefruit, the heart beats 60–80 times a minute. This rises to over 100 during vigorous exercise.

Circulation

Blood acts as a transport system. Each drop contains 250 million red blood cells which ferry food and oxygen around the body and remove waste. Each day, 170 billion blood cells are produced, while 2 million die every second. The heart pumps blood through arteries so that it reaches every organ in the body. If all the body's blood vessels were laid out end to end, they would be 160,000km long.

CIRCLE LINE
Arteries (red) circulate blood rich in oxygen. Veins (blue) take oxygen-poor blood to the heart and lungs.

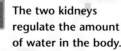

When blood reaches the lungs, it takes in fresh oxygen that we have just breathed in, and releases a waste gas, carbon dioxide, which we then breathe out. The blood carries the oxygen and food from the stomach to every cell in the body.

When the body is resting, it takes about a minute for the blood to make one circuit of the body.

DATABANK

INPUT	OUTPUT
Q How many litres of blood are there flowing in the body?	**A** Adults have about 5 litres of blood. This would half fill a bucket.
Q How many kidneys are there and what are they used for?	**A** The two kidneys regulate the amount of water in the body.
Q What's the difference between white and red blood cells?	**A** Red cells carry oxygen and food; white cells defend against germs.
Q What happens to the body when the heart stops beating?	**A** Without blood, body tissues die. The brain is affected first.

Brain

The brain is the body's control centre. It enables us to move, to think and to learn, and is far more powerful than the most complex computer. Although the brain accounts for only 2 per cent of the body's weight, it needs 20 per cent of the body's blood. It sends messages to the body along nerves, which act like telephone wires. Moving at 320 km/h, these impulses tell muscles to move, instruct the heart to pump and ensure that we keep breathing. Impulses also carry information from every part of the body back to the brain.

THE SENSES

The senses give us all our information about the outside world. They enable us to see and touch our surroundings, to hear what is being said to us and to smell and taste what we eat.

Sight

Sight is the most complex sense. When we look at something, light from that object enters our eyes. The cornea and lens focus the light on to the 130 million light-sensitive cells in the retina at the back of the eye. These cells are split into two groups: the rods detect general shape and movement and the cones detect detail and colour. The image that forms is upside down, but the information is sent via the optic nerve to the brain, which correctly interprets the image.

Optic nerve   Retina

Lens
Iris
Cornea
Pupil

Touch

The touch-sensitive nerve endings embedded in our skin are the most widespread of the sense organs, covering the whole of the body. There are five main types of touch receptor, each detecting a different form of sensation. Merkel and Meissner sensors detect light touch while Pacini and Rufini sensors detect pressure. Free nerve endings detect a wider range of sensations and react to pain.

A fly's eyes react much faster than a human's. At a cinema, a fly could see the individual frames of a movie.

Taste and smell

Our senses of taste and smell are closely linked. They work by detecting chemicals in food and in the air, and so are also known as the chemosenses. In some animals, the two senses are combined – snakes use their tongues to taste for scents in the air. Our sense of taste is limited to four basic chemical reactions. This is compensated for by our ability to detect over 10,000 different smell chemicals, which enhance our impression of the taste of food in our mouth. Children have a more acute sense of smell than adults, but this sense slowly weakens with age as the smell receptors die off.

Some people have synaesthesia. This means that their senses are confused – a sound may be interpreted as a colour!

Bitter

Sweet

Sour

Salt

TASTE BUDS
The tongue has over 10,000 taste buds, but can only identify four tastes – salt, sour, sweet and bitter. Each taste is detected by the taste buds located in a specific area of the tongue.

Sound travels in waves. The number of sound waves each second is called its frequency and is measured in hertz.

Fish have a different sense. A line of nerves along the side of their body detects vibrations in the water.

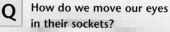

DATABANK

Q How do we move our eyes in their sockets?

A Each eyeball is attached to six sets of muscles, which control its direction of gaze.

Q Which areas of the body are most sensitive to touch?

A The face, mouth, hands and feet have the largest number of touch receptors in the body.

Hearing

Our sense of hearing can detect a very wide range of sound frequencies – from deep rumbling noises at 30 hertz to high-pitched squeals at 18,000 hertz. Sound enters the outer ear and vibrates the eardrum. Sensitive hairs within the cochlea (about 240,000 of them) convert these vibrations into electrical signals. The signals are sent along nerve paths to the brain, where they are interpreted as sounds.

SOUND SENSE
Bats use a form of sonar. By listening for the echoes of their squeaks they can locate their prey in the dark.

Nerve

Cochlea

Semicircular canals

TUBEWAY
The ear is linked to the throat by the Eustachian tube. It relieves damaging build-ups of pressure within the ear.

Ear canal

Eardrum

Pinna (gathers sounds)

MEDICINE

Today, people are living longer than ever. Treatments have been found for some 'incurable' diseases and expert surgery saves millions of lives each year.

Disease

Before the 20th century, serious infectious diseases, such as smallpox and diphtheria, were usually fatal. Caused by organisms that attack the body, such as bacteria, they spread easily from person to person. Today, drugs and improved hygiene have eradicated or contained many of the worst types. Now, the biggest killers are non-infectious diseases, such as cancer. In the developed world, these kill 1,000 per 100,000 people, compared to 5 per 100,000 people for infectious diseases.

MOSQUITO MENACE
The malaria virus is carried by mosquitos which spread the disease to humans. Malaria kills over a million people a year.

Diseases of the heart and blood account for over 50 per cent of deaths in developed Western nations.

BLACK DEATH
Carried by rat fleas, bubonic plague (the Black Death) killed up to half of Europe's population in the mid-1300s.

COUGHS AND SNEEZES
Up to 22 million people died in the influenza (flu) epidemic that struck worldwide after World War I.

Diagnosis

Doctors have existed for thousands of years. For example, the *Code of Hammurabi* from Babylon, 1800BC, is a text relating to medical practice. Many people believed that illnesses were punishments and could only be cured using magic. Ancient Greek physicians, such as Hippocrates, challenged this. He used observation and logic to understand illnesses and provide effective treatment. His methods form the basis of medical practice today. Yet the Greeks did not permit experiments on dead bodies. It was hundreds of years later that men like William Harvey (1578–1657) learned how the body worked by dissecting animals and humans. Harvey discovered how the blood circulates.

Andreas Vesalius (1514–64) of Belgium studied human anatomy using the bodies of executed criminals.

AHEAD OF HIS TIME
Hippocrates (about 460–377BC) believed that fresh air, exercise and cleanliness were vital for health – just like we do today!

ASPIRIN
The Ancient Egyptians used tea made from willow bark, which contains aspirin, to relieve pain.

HIPPOCRATIS COI
Gemina effigies ex antiquo numismate graeco Constantinopoli reperto

48

ROSY PERIWINKLE
Once thought to be worthless, the rosy periwinkle from Madagascar's rainforests is used in drugs for treating leukemia.

Vaccines

British doctor Edward Jenner (1749–1823) discovered the first vaccine. He noticed that people who had suffered from cowpox did not catch deadly smallpox. To test this, he infected a boy with cowpox before exposing him to smallpox. The boy remained healthy – by fighting off the milder disease, his body had built up defences against smallpox. Using this knowledge, scientists created a smallpox vaccine that was eventually used worldwide. It was so successful that by 1979, the disease had been eliminated.

THE ANTIBIOTIC MAN
British scientist Alexander Fleming discovered penicillin in 1928. It is used to treat diseases caused by bacteria.

BRAIN SCAN
Modern scanners can 'see' deep inside the body and even look at the brain in detail, showing up problems.

FACTS AND FIGURES

The AIDS virus was discovered in 1984 by French scientist Luc Montaigner.

The first successful heart transplant was performed in South Africa in 1967.

Blood transfusions were attempted in Italy in the 1600s but were later banned.

French chemist Louis Pasteur (1822–95) developed vaccines for anthrax and rabies.

Surgical breakthroughs

Operations were so dangerous 150 years ago that most people died. Shock was a big killer, so doctors gave their patients anaesthetics to numb pain, such as wine and laughing gas! Even when effective anaesthetics were used, patients still died. Scottish surgeon Joseph Lister (1828–1912) realized that germs were the problem. After he ordered that everything, including the doctors, must be kept scrupulously clean, fewer people died. Another major breakthrough came with the first use of the heart-lung machine in 1953. A heart could be stopped while the machine took over, giving surgeons time to operate. In the 1960s, surgeons began transplanting hearts and other organs.

DATABANK

INPUT   **OUTPUT**

Q What is the most dangerous threat to health today?

A Tobacco-related illnesses are the most urgent health problem.

Q Are many diseases prevented with vaccines?

A Vaccines exist for polio, measles, influenza and many more.

Q How many people are affected by cancer worldwide?

A 25 per cent of people in the developed world, less elsewhere.

Q Who discovered X-rays and when?

A German Wilhelm Röentgen discovered X-rays in 1895.

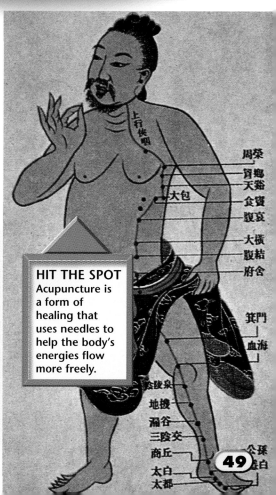

HIT THE SPOT
Acupuncture is a form of healing that uses needles to help the body's energies flow more freely.

ATHLETICS

Athletics is divided into two areas: field events, which include long jump, high jump, discus, javelin and shot put; and track events, which involve running over various distances.

The Olympics

Held every four years, the Olympic Games, with athletics at its core, is the world's greatest sports event. The Games began at Olympia in ancient Greece, and records of it exist from as early as 776BC. It was a religious festival, but winning was very important. The modern Olympics began in Athens, Greece in 1896, instigated by Frenchman Pierre de Coubertin. He believed that competition and exercise in the form of sports and games were vital for all. However, it was not until 1928 that women were officially allowed to compete. In ancient times, winners received an olive wreath but today they are awarded a gold medal.

RINGS OF PEACE
The Olympic rings represent the five inhabited continents and symbolize the international nature of the modern Games.

PASS IT ON
Each member of a relay team runs part of the race, passing the baton on to a team-mate at the end of the run.

Roman emperor Theodosius I prohibited pagan worship in AD393. This included the Olympic Games!

On your marks

Running events range from the 100m to the marathon, which is about 42.2km. Sprinters, such as the USA's Maurice Greene and Marion Jones (winners of the men's and women's 100m at the World Championships in 1999) use power and pure speed. Long-distance runners rely more on stamina. African runners, such as Ethiopia's Haile Gebrselassie, regularly dominate events over 800m.

MILE HIGH
In 1954, Britain's Roger Bannister became the first man to run a mile (1609.3m) in less than four minutes. Today, athletes train harder than ever and the world record is 17 seconds quicker!

HASSIBA BOULMERKA
This great Algerian athlete won the 1,500m in 1991 in Tokyo – becoming the first African woman to win a world title.

GREAT BRIT
The greatest British 100m runner ever, Linford Christie won the Olympic title in 1992 and the World title in 1993. He lost his Olympic title in 1996 to Canada's Donovan Bailey.

Field events

Field events, comprising jumping and throwing disciplines, take place in the space within the running track. In field events, technique is as important as power and strength. For example, in the high jump, competitors must have perfect timing to transfer their run-up speed into jumping height. In the javelin, the winner is the person with the best throwing action. Jan Zelezny of the Czech Republic has perfected the javelin in the 1990s. His throw of 98.48m in 1996 remains an almost impossible target for his rivals. The javelin event also appeared at the ancient Olympics and derived from soldiers' spear-throwing contests.

The decathlon is an event where athletes compete over ten different track and field disciplines.

CARL LEWIS
Lewis won four gold medals at the Los Angeles Olympics, 1984: the long jump, 100m, 200m and 100m relay.

UP AND OVER
Before it became a sport, pole vaulting was an effective method for crossing ditches and fences.

FACTS AND FIGURES

Overall, the USA has won more Olympic gold medals than any other country – 833.

Romanian Lia Manoliu (36) won the discus in 1968 – the oldest female Olympic winner.

Ed Moses (USA) won 122 consecutive 400m hurdle races between 1977 and 1987.

Merlene Ottey, the Jamaican sprinter, has won a record 14 World Championship medals.

Maurice Greene ran the 100m in a record 9.79 seconds in Athens, 16 June 1999.

Bob Beamon's long jump world record, set in 1968, was not broken until 1991.

Tegla Loroupe of Kenya ran the women's marathon in a record 2:20.23 hours in 1999.

FINE SHOT
China's Xinmei Sui won a silver medal in the shot put at the 1998 Olympics. The shot used to be a real cannon ball – hence the event's name. The Ancient Greeks used a heavy stone.

TEAM SPORTS

Many team sports began as disorganized games, with little thought of rules. Over time, as more people played the games, they evolved into the familiar sports we know today.

Bat and ball

Sports involving a bat and ball have been played throughout history. There is even evidence to suggest that the Ancient Greeks and Egyptians played a game with a ball and stick. In England, cricket was probably played as early as 1300. It was the first game to evolve a set of fixed rules, with written copies dating back to 1744. In the USA, the most popular bat and ball game is baseball. Based loosely on the English game of rounders, the rules of baseball were developed by Alexander Cartwright in 1845. Native Americans played their own bat and ball game, called baggataway, which prepared their young warriors for the trials of hunting.

GOOD GRACE
One of the finest cricketers ever seen, Dr W. G. Grace (England) played for 44 years and scored over 54,000 runs.

BASKETBALL
The tallest ever basketball player, at 2.45m, was Sulieman Ali Nashnush of Libya's 1962 national team.

The soccer World Cup trophy was stolen in 1966, but was later found under a bush by a dog called Pickles.

Teamwork

Some team sports were developed to build fitness. In 1891, a Canadian clergyman and teacher, Dr James Naismith, invented basketball as a means of making exercise more fun. His students enjoyed the game so much that news of it soon spread to other colleges. Today, the sport is played all over the world. Rugby union is a team sport that encourages both teamwork and rivalry. The annual match between the English universities of Oxford and Cambridge is keenly fought, and the Six Nations Championships, played between England, Ireland, Scotland, Wales, France and Italy is one of sport's most fiercely contested competitions.

OARS RACING
Oxford and Cambridge universities compete each year in the Boat Race along the River Thames.

FACTS AND FIGURES

The Boston Celtics have won the most NBA basketball championships – 16.

Australian Jeff Thomson bowled the fastest cricket ball ever – at 160 km/h.

Wales have been rugby union champions of Europe most often.

In the first Superbowl, 1967, the Green Bay Packers beat the Kansas City Chiefs 35–10.

Australia has won the Rugby League World Cup a record seven times.

West Indian Brian Lara holds the highest individual test cricket score – 375 not out.

The New York Yankees have won the baseball World Series a record 23 times.

FALLEN HERO
Diego Maradona led Argentina to the 1986 soccer World Cup, scoring one of the best goals ever seen in the quarter-final. But he was expelled from the 1994 competition for drug-taking.

HOME RUN
American, Mark McGwire scored 70 home runs in the 1998 baseball season, setting an all time record.

Soccer

Soccer is one of the oldest sports in the world. Some believe that it originated in the Far East, where victorious soldiers would kick around the severed heads of defeated enemies. In England, basic versions of the game were banned by several kings because of the violence involved. The modern game evolved in the second half of the 19th century due to its popularity in schools. One of the most famous teams playing today is the English club Manchester United, with supporters world-wide. Achieving a rare treble in 1999, the team won the English Premier league, the F. A. Cup and the European Champions Cup.

American football

Derived from a mixture of the English games of rugby and soccer, American football was played first in schools and universities before becoming a professional sport in 1920. The premier match is the Superbowl, held annually between the season's two most successful teams. It is one of the most popular television events of the year in the USA, watched by an average of 138 million people. First won in 1967 by the Green Bay Packers, the Superbowl has since been won a record five times each by the Dallas Cowboys and the San Francisco Forty-Niners.

Pele, the world's greatest soccer player, scored 1,281 goals in 21 years and won three World Cup medals.

LONG RUN
Desmond Howard (US) of the Green Bay Packers won the most valuable player award during the 1997 Superbowl, for his 99-yard kick off return. He ran nearly a full pitch length.

SOLO SPORTS

In some sports, success depends on players working as a team. In others, however, it is up to the individual to find reserves of strength, courage and skill to beat all opponents and set new personal goals.

WINNER
Although a UK competition, Wimbledon has not been won by a British man since Fred Perry's victory in 1936.

Tennis

Tennis can be traced back to the French king's court in the 12th century. The modern game was adopted by the All-England Lawn Tennis and Croquet Club in 1877, when the Wimbledon tournament first took place. German Boris Becker became the youngest man to triumph at Wimbledon when he won the singles in 1987 at the age of 17. Great modern champions include the USA's Martina Navratilova and Pete Sampras with 8 and 6 singles titles respectively.

TRIUMPH
Germany's Steffi Graf won all four major tennis tournaments, known as the Grand Slam titles, in 1988.

Golf

The sport of badminton is named after the Duke of Beaufort's house. He invented the game in 1873.

Golf was played in Scotland as far back as the 15th century, but the first amateur championship was held in 1885. Today the four main golf titles are all professional competitions. These are: the British Open, the US Open, the US PGA and the US Masters championships – collectively known as the Majors. American golfing legend Jack Nicklaus is the only player to have won every Major twice. Known as the 'Golden Bear', Nicklaus won a total of 18 Major championships.

BOBBY JONES
In 1930, this great American golfer won all four US and British Open and Amateur Championships.

DATABANK

Q What is the world's premier cycling competition?

A Established in 1903, the Tour de France brings together the world's best riders.

Q What age was the youngest Formula One motor racing champion?

A Brazilian Emerson Fittipaldi won the title at the age of 25 years and nine months in 1972.

SWINGER
Eldrick 'Tiger' Woods (US) became the youngest person to win the US Masters in 1997 at the age of 21. It is claimed that he swung his first golf club when he was just 11 months old.

FAST FERRARI
Ferrari are the most successful Formula One team, winning 125 Grand Prix victories by the end of the 1999 Season.

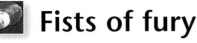

Speed masters

The first motor race took place in France in 1894, shortly after the invention of the car. Early races were so dangerous that most were moved to specially designed tracks. The average speed of these first races was 20 km/h, today cars reach speeds of over 200 km/h. The major titles include the Indy Car series in the USA, with the Indianapolis 500 as its highlight, and the Formula One World Championship – fought over a season of 15 or 16 races.

IRON MIKE
American Mike Tyson, shown here with the UK's Frank Bruno, was one of the most feared boxers.

Fists of fury

Boxing was one of the original sports at the Olympic games in Ancient Greece. The Romans also used a form of boxing during gladiator fights to the death. In 1867, the 'Queensberry rules' on which modern boxing is based, were adopted to make the sport safer. Muhammad Ali of the USA was one of the world's greatest and most charismatic boxers. After winning an Olympic title in 1960, Ali turned professional, becoming world heavyweight champion three times before retiring – a record.

Most boxers fight in categories that are determined by their weight – from flyweight to heavyweight.

FACTS AND FIGURES

UK tennis player Greg Rusedski can hit a tennis ball at up to 239 km/h.

The horse *Red Rum* won the English Grand National horse race a record three times.

At 45, Hale Irwin became the oldest player to win the US Open golf championship.

Argentina's Juan-Manuel Fangio won the Formula One driver's title five times.

US heavyweight boxer Rocky Marciano won all of his 49 professional fights.

EPSOM DERBY
Held since 1780, the Derby at Epsom in the UK is one of the most important and famous events of the horse-racing year.

WINTER SPORTS

Sporting competition is not restricted to the summer months – even in the snow and ice people still challenge each other to master the hostile winter conditions.

 ## On the slopes

The oldest skis have been found in Scandinavia and date back 5,000 years. These were not used for sport but as a reliable form of transport on snow. The modern sport of skiing is split into two rival traditions. 'Nordic' skiing includes cross-country skiing, biathlon and ski-jumping while 'alpine' skiing focuses more on downhill and slalom events. In the men's Nordic events, Norwegian Bjørn Dæhlie reigns supreme, winning eight Olympic medals since 1992 and a further six World Cup titles. In alpine disciplines, Vreni Schneider of Switzerland won all seven women's World Cup slalom titles in the 1988–89 season. Austrian Franz Klammer has won five men's World Cup downhill titles, while Luxembourg's Marc Giradelli has equalled this achievement in a range of alpine events. Skiing is still evolving, with variations like snowboarding becoming popular.

A slope of compacted snow that is used to host skiing events is called the piste.

BORN TO FLY
Finnish ski jumper, Matti Nykänen has won a record four Olympic titles. He is pictured here winning gold in the 90m event at the Calgary Olympics in Canada in 1988.

DATABANK

Q Where and when were the first Winter Olympics held?

A In Chamonix, France in 1924, although they were not officially recognized as such until 1925.

Q What is the Cresta Run and why is it famous?

A It is a 1,213m long sled-run in Switzerland. Competitions have been held there since 1885.

OLYMPIAN
Jean-Luc Cretier of France won gold in the men's downhill event at the 1998 Winter Olympics in Nagano, Japan.

FACTS AND FIGURES

Germany's Katrina Witt won Olympic and World figure skating titles in 1984 and 1988.

The fastest speed reached by a skater is 248 km/h by Austria's Harry Egger in 1999.

Australia beat New Zealand 58–nil at ice hockey in 1987 – the most goals ever scored.

Ski designer Sondre Nordheim won the first ski jumping competition in 1866.

Georg Hackl of Germany has won a record six World Championship luge titles.

By the end of 1998, Karine Ruby of France had won 11 snowboarding world titles.

Ice hockey

Played since the mid-18th century, ice hockey is a mixture of Native American games and the sport of hockey. In Canada, where it is hugely popular, the sport was originally played outside, with the first indoor rink opening in 1875. Today, most teams have their own indoor venue. The Canadian National Hockey League (NHL), in which teams compete for the Stanley Cup, is one of the world's best.

With players moving at speeds of up to 50 km/h, ice hockey is the fastest team sport in the world.

GIVING THEM STICK
Known as 'The Great One', Canadian Wayne Gretzky scored 1,072 goals in his 20-year career.

ICE BULLET
In the luge, competitors wear rubber suits to reduce wind resistance. They travel at up to 100 km/h.

SKATES ON
A full Olympic sport since 1994, short-track speed skating requires great skill. Groups of skaters race each other at close quarters around a tight 111m track.

Bobsledding

Winter sports involving a sled date from the 16th century. Bobsledding, where a manned sled speeds down an ice-covered slope, emerged at the end of the 19th century. Taking its name from the bobbing movement of the riders – which was used to increase speed – the modern sport is divided into two- and four-man events. Switzerland is the premier bobsledding nation and has won the World four-man title 20 times.

CHEMISTRY

Chemistry is the study of what things are made from. This involves examining how elements and compounds behave and how they react with other substances.

Elements and compounds

The world around us is made up of a limited number of chemical elements. Scientists have discovered 109 of these and each has different properties. Yet 98 per cent of Earth's crust is made up of just eight elements, including oxygen, iron, aluminium, sodium and calcium. Elements often combine to form new substances – called compounds – of which there are millions. Water is a compound of oxygen and hydrogen, while salt is a compound of sodium and chlorine.

BUCKYBALL
Buckyballs, or fullerenes, are the third form of pure carbon known to exist after graphite and diamond.

SOLID LIQUID?
The surface of a liquid acts like a stretchy skin. It is strong enough to hold very light things like this pond skater.

Altered states

Matter exists in three states – gas, liquid or solid. In a solid object, the particles are tightly bonded together and cannot move. In a liquid, these bonds are looser and the molecules move freely against each other. In a gas, the bonds between molecules are completely broken. There is nothing to stop the substance spreading out to fill the space it is in.

At room temperature, 2 elements are liquid, 96 are solids and 11 are gases.

Gas
If water is heated to 100°C, its molecules move quickly and break their bonds. Water becomes a gas (steam).

Liquid
Between 1°C and 99°C, water is a liquid. The bonds between molecules are loose. Liquids change shape to fit their containers.

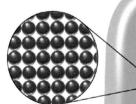

Solid
If water is cooled to 0°C or below, the molecules bond together tightly in a solid known as ice.

WEIRD WATER
Water has baffled scientists because as a solid (ice) it is less dense than when it is a liquid – unlike all other solids.

Chemical reactions

Chemical reactions occur all around us and are the means by which new substances are created from existing ones. For example, water is created when hydrogen and oxygen are ignited together. When a chemical reaction occurs, the bonds between molecules break, enabling elements to combine with each other to form compounds. Reactions are used to produce many items, including soap, drugs, cosmetics, paint and plastic. Reactions even occur within our bodies. The oxygen that we breathe in reacts with glucose (a sugar compound containing hydrogen, carbon and oxygen) from our food to produce energy, water and a waste gas called carbon dioxide. We use up the energy and water and breathe out the carbon dioxide (a compound of carbon and oxygen). Heat speeds up a reaction. For example, if you hold an iron pan over a strong flame, rust will form more quickly than normal.

FACTS AND FIGURES

Helium melts at –272°C while carbon in the form of diamond melts at 3500°C.

90 per cent of matter in the Universe is hydrogen. It is also the lightest element.

The rarest natural element is astatine. Less than 0.5g of this is present in Earth's crust.

The first elements to be discovered were metals, used since prehistoric times.

The heaviest naturally occurring element is uranium. It is used in nuclear reactions.

The lightest metal is lithium. It weighs about half as much as water, so it floats!

When iron (a solid metal) is heated to over 1539°C, it becomes a liquid.

Water has one oxygen atom and two hydrogen atoms. Its chemical formula is H_2O.

EVERYDAY CHEMISTRY
Cement is vital in building. The chemicals within it react with water, making it harden and stick objects together.

When iron is mixed with carbon, it becomes extra hard. The new substance is called steel.

CORROSION
Rust is made when the metal iron reacts with the gas oxygen. This creates iron oxide. The reaction is very slow.

DATABANK

INPUT

Q How many elements exist naturally and how many have been created artificially?

Q Who are alchemists and are they similar to chemists?

Q What is the Periodic Table?

Q Who was the first person to discover how chemical reactions worked?

OUTPUT

A There are 95 naturally occurring elements. 14 more have been created in laboratories.

A In the past, alchemists tried to turn ordinary metal into gold. Their experiments were the beginning of chemistry.

A The Periodic Table is an attempt to arrange the elements in order, relating to the size of their atoms.

A Frenchman Antoine Lavoisier (1743–94) examined reactions by studying the role of oxygen in burning.

PHYSICS

Physics tries to explain how the Universe works. Physicists study everything from very small things, such as atoms, to unbelievably large things, such as solar systems.

AIR FORCE
After being heated, air rises and pushes against the fabric of a balloon, pushing it upwards against the pull of gravity.

Forces

A force is something that pushes or pulls an object in a particular direction. When you throw a ball or lift a weight, you exert a force on the object. The English scientist Isaac Newton (1642–1727) discovered that if an object exerts a force on another, it receives an equal and opposite force in return. For example, if you rollerskate up to a wall and push it you move off in the opposite direction – the wall 'pushes' you back! Confusingly, forces can also keep things standing still. You might expect a car to roll down any slope – the force of gravity (see below) normally pulls it down. However, if the slope is very slight, another type of force between the car's tyres and the slope stops it moving. This force is called friction. The friction between the soles of your shoes and the floor enables you to grip the ground. Without it, you might slip over.

POTENTIAL
When a spring is pulled back, such as in pinball, it is ready to exert a force. It has what is called *potential energy*.

BOUNCER
A tennis ball falls pulled by gravity. As it hits the ground, it receives an equal force and bounces up.

FACTS AND FIGURES

Electric current is measured in amps – after French physicist André Ampère (1775–1836).

Italian Alexandro Volta (1745–1827) made the first battery in 1800.

Ernest Rutherford, a scientist from New Zealand, first split an atom in 1919.

The word atom comes from the Greek word *atomos*, which means 'uncut'.

An atom is thought to be about 0.00000001cm wide.

Friction is strongest between objects with rough surfaces.

SHAPED FOR FLIGHT
A wing is shaped so that air pressure is higher beneath it than above it. This sucks up the wing.

Gravity

Objects exert a force of attraction towards each other, which is known as gravity. The larger the object's mass (the amount of matter it contains), the greater the attraction. Earth's mass is so huge, it pulls everything nearby towards it. The Sun's gravity is even greater and keeps the planets in orbit around it. The Moon's gravity pulls the water around in the oceans, causing tides.

BEATING GRAVITY
To stay in the air, planes need lift from their wings and forward thrust to balance the friction of the air.

Magnetism

Magnets attract materials containing iron, cobalt or nickel and have two poles – north and south. The first law of magnetism is that like poles repel each other and opposite poles attract. All magnets are surrounded by a magnetic field. This area consists of invisible lines that go from the north to south poles of a magnet. Englishman Michael Faraday (1791–1867) discovered that magnetic fields are closely related to electricity (see below).

N

S

COMPASS
Earth is like a huge bar magnet, with a north and south pole. A compass contains a tiny magnet that is attracted to Earth's north pole. This helps travellers to find their way.

Axle – allows coil to rotate

Wire coil (magnetized)

Fixed magnet (north)

Fixed magnet (south)

Electric current introduced here

Electricity

Electricity is a form of energy produced by the movement of invisible particles. Faraday noticed that when a wire is moved between two magnets, particles flow along the wire making an electrical current. These currents provide us with a versatile and clean form of energy. We use it to drive motors (left), produce light and make powerful electromagnets.

ELECTRIC MOTOR
An electric current turns a wire coil into a magnet. Fixed magnets 'repel' the coil and cause it to spin – creating a motor.

ATOM BOMB
An atom bomb splits billions of atom nuclei at the same time, creating a chain reaction and a huge explosion.

Atoms

Atoms are the building blocks of the Universe. Everything around us is made up of atoms. An atom has a centre called a nucleus surrounded by particles called electrons. The nucleus is made up of particles called protons and neutrons. Scientists can split the nucleus of an atom. This starts off a chain reaction, which can release a vast amount of heat and energy – the basis for nuclear power.

INSIDE THE BOMB
This contains several pieces of radioactive material that react when brought together, causing their atoms to split.

NUCLEAR REACTOR
This power plant produces energy by splitting atoms. The energy drives generators, which produce electricity.

INVENTIONS

An invention is a new item or technique created by humans. Inventors take existing knowledge and use it in a different way. Many inventions have changed the way we live.

Full steam ahead

Boiling water creates steam. By carefully channelling steam, engineers realized that it could be used as energy to drive a machine. In 1698, Thomas Savery designed an engine to pump water out of mines – a design improved by Thomas Newcomen and, later, James Watt. Steam was eventually used to power locomotives and ships.

ROTARY STEAM ENGINE
Scotsman James Watt's rotary steam engine became a major source of power for industry, particularly in large factories.

The home

Michael Faraday discovered how to generate electricity in 1831, but it was years before it had a practical use in the home. By the early 1900s, inventors had designed electrical appliances, such as irons, vacuum cleaners and kettles, which saved time and energy. Many people who had used servants to look after their houses now did their own chores!

IRON
Irons used to be heated over a fire. The first electric irons were dangerous. Safer versions arrived in 1882.

SQUEEZE DRY
The first washing machine was designed by American James King in 1851. It was powered by hand.

FACTS AND FIGURES

Hero of Alexandria created a primitive steam engine in the 1st century AD.

American Christopher Sholes created the first efficient typewriter in 1868.

Englishman Sir John Harrington designed the first flushing toilet in 1596.

Thomas Edison held a world record 1,093 patents, either singly or jointly.

As well as inventing the telephone, Alexander Bell experimented with flight!

The first public telephone systems were in use by 1880.

A discovery, like electricity, is not an invention. It has always existed but was only 'found' recently.

LIGHT BULB
Britain's Joseph Swan exhibited an electric light in 1860. He was followed 20 years later by US inventor, Thomas Edison. The two men developed a practical light bulb in 1880.

Telephone

Scotsman Alexander Graham Bell invented the telephone in 1876. His work with the deaf led him to examine how sound vibrates in air. He found that electrical currents could be altered to resemble the vibrations of the voice. With his assistant, Thomas Watson, he built the 'Box Telephone'.

PHONE BOX
Bell's telephone converted the voice into an electrical current which could be sent along wires to a receiver.

Thomas Alva Edison

The American genius Thomas Edison (1847–1931) was one of the most influential inventors of all. His first inventions came about through his work as a telegraph operator. Being partially deaf, he created a printer that converted electrical signals from sound to letters. In 1877, he invented the phonograph, a means of recording the human voice. By 1880, his light bulb was a success. In 1893, he built the first motion picture stage. He also produced the alkali battery for storing and supplying electricity.

At first, some experts believed that Edison's phonograph was merely a ventriloquist's trick.

GROOVY
The phonograph recorded sounds onto grooves on a foil cylinder. The sounds were replayed when a needle hit the grooves. German Emil Berliner replaced the cylinder with a flat disc in 1904.

FROM VINYL TO DISC
Compact discs store sounds so that they can be read by lasers. Introduced in the 1980s, they are more durable than vinyl.

CAMERA
The camera was invented in the 1820s. Frenchman Joseph-Nicéphore Niepce took the first photo in 1827.

Progress

The 20th century has seen many innovations. In 1914, Alfred Benesch invented automatic traffic lights – proof that the motor car was becoming a success. Robert Watson-Watt's discovery of radar in 1935 revolutionized warfare, while Jacques Cousteau's aqualung (1943) opened up the underwater world. Today, inventors try to create machines that cost less, use energy efficiently and minimize damage to the environment.

DATABANK

Q Who invented the wheel, and when and where did they live?

A People living in Mesopotamia (modern-day Iraq) invented the wheel in about 3000BC.

Q What is a patent and why does an inventor need to have one?

A It is a legal document that prevents other people from copying an inventor's design.

THE *TURTLE*
This US one-man submarine was used to attack British warships in the War of Independence in 1776.

STATE OF THE ART
The first film cameras were big, unwieldy instruments. Today, people can make movies with a hand-held camcorder.

FLYING BEDSTEAD
This strange machine was designed in the UK to test vertical take-offs. It led to the development of the jump jet.

COMMUNICATION

Over the last 100 years, sending and receiving messages has become faster and easier. However, new technology in the form of the Internet looks set to change the way we communicate with each other.

Television and radio

Radio and TV technology works by turning sounds or pictures into radio waves. The waves are then transmitted through the air or along cables to radios and TV sets that convert the waves back into sounds and pictures for us to understand. As it is easy to reach people with radio waves, radio and TV are the most powerful forms of mass communication.

FIBRE OPTICS
Fibre optics are very efficient. They use light rather than radio waves to transmit sound and pictures.

It is thought that the average person in the UK will spend two years of his or her life watching TV.

VISION ON
The Scottish scientist John Logie Baird demonstrated his 'scanning-disc' television set in 1926.

Satellite

Man-made satellites are unmanned spacecraft that orbit Earth. Once information, such as phone conversations or TV pictures, is beamed up to them they broadcast it over vast distances. Some satellites move at the same speed as Earth rotates so that they remain over the same point of Earth's surface at all times. The oldest satellite in orbit is *Vanguard 1*, which was launched by the USA in 1958.

Smoke signals and flags provided long-distance communication before radio waves were discovered.

FACTS AND FIGURES

Italian physicist and inventor Guglielmo Marconi developed the first radio in 1895.

It is estimated that there are at least two radios per person in the USA.

China has between 230 and 250 million television sets. Its total population is 1.1 billion.

The first electronic computer was built in the USA in 1945. It weighed 30 tonnes.

Super Mario Brothers has sold 40 million copies – the best-selling computer game ever.

US company Compaq, the biggest PC manufacturer, sold over 13 million PCs in 1998.

SENSOR
The European Remote Sensing satellite detects changes in Earth's crust and helps predict earthquakes.

SKY SCAN
The Space Shuttle scans Earth while in orbit, looking for natural resources. It gives us a far clearer picture of Earth's surface than we would get from the ground.

In 1997, a computer, IBM's *Deep Blue*, beat a world chess champion, Garry Kasparov, for the first time.

Computers

A computer is an electronic device that can do calculations millions of times faster than a human. Early computers filled whole rooms, but the invention of the microchip meant that thousands of parts could be fitted onto a piece of silicon just 5mm square. Today computers are as common as cars. Easy to understand, they are used in many areas of life, such as 'surfing' the Internet, designing books, playing games and even controlling space missions!

GAME ON
PCs are ideal for playing games. Car racing simulations, such as *The Streets of Sim City*, are always popular.

MICROCHIP
Crammed with tiny wires and transistors, microchips replaced bulky electronic circuits and reduced the size of computers.

BABBAGE'S ENGINE
Charles Babbage invented a calculating device in the 1820s. He is regarded as the father of the modern computer.

Internet

The Internet is an international network of computers that link businesses and individuals. More people are connecting to the 'Net' every day and by the start of 1999, there were 150 million users. This will become 400 million by the end of 2000 as more people use it to shop, bank, find information or play games. One Internet game, *Ultima Online,* has up to 14,000 people playing at the same time!

WORLD WIDE WEB
A PC connected to the Internet can view web pages from – and send e-mails to – almost anywhere in the world!

DATABANK

INPUT

Q What are radio waves and when were they first discovered?

Q How does a mobile phone work?

Q Who started the Internet or World Wide Web, and when did it all begin?

Q What are computer viruses? Are they contagious and can I catch them?

OUTPUT

A They are a type of electromagnetic radiation similar to X-rays. They were first discovered in 1873.

A Mobile phones transmit their signals along microwaves beamed over an area by local radio transmitters.

A The Internet began in the 1960s as a US experiment to find a communication system to survive a nuclear war.

A These are computer programs that deliberately damage other files. They spread only from computer to computer!

STRUCTURES OF OLD

Throughout history, people have erected great buildings and monuments to glorify their gods and kings, and to proclaim their wealth and strength to their neighbours. This led to the creation of many fabulous structures.

Seven Wonders

In the 2nd century BC, the writer Antipater of Sidon compiled a list of the most famous and impressive buildings, monuments and statues known to the Ancient World. The list became known as the Seven Wonders of the World. Even today, architects marvel at the skill that was used to create these impressive structures – especially as the people who made them had no computers, mechanical cranes or digging machines to help them. Sadly, most of the Seven Wonders are now in ruins or, like the Hanging Gardens of Babylon and the Colossus of Rhodes, have disappeared completely. However, the Pyramids of Giza in Egypt have changed little throughout the ages and still inspire awe in all who see them.

The only Wonders still intact today – the pyramids – are also the oldest and date from 2600–2500BC.

STATUE OF ZEUS
Erected by Phidias of Athens at Olympus in 430BC in honour of the king of the gods.

COLOSSUS
A 40m tall bronze statue of the Sun god Helios, which was erected on Rhodes in 290BC.

MAUSOLEUM
Built as the tomb for King Mausolus of Caria (now in Turkey) by his wife in 353BC.

PHAROS
A huge lighthouse, 140m tall, that was built in about 280BC to protect shipping entering the port of Alexandria.

GARDENS
Nebuchadnezzar, king of Babylon, built the Hanging Gardens for his wife in 580BC.

TEMPLE
Built in the 6th century BC, the Temple of Artemis (in modern Turkey) had 100 columns.

GREAT PYRAMIDS OF GIZA
The pyramids were gigantic tombs for the pharaohs – the kings of Egypt. The Pyramids of Giza are the biggest.

Historical buildings

The Egyptians, Greeks and Romans built on a vast scale. Some of their most famous buildings, such as the Acropolis in Athens, were erected in honour of the gods. During the Middle Ages and Renaissance, buildings in Europe were also dominated by religion. St Peter's in Rome, which was rebuilt in the 16th century, remained the world's largest Christian church until 1989, when it was superseded by the basilica in Yamoussoukro in the Ivory Coast. Defence also influenced building in ancient times. The Great Wall of China, which is about 6,400km long, was built in 221–206BC to protect China from invaders. If it was straightened out, it would be long enough to reach across the Atlantic Ocean from the British Isles to Canada.

DEFENCE
The art of castle building was at its height in the Middle Ages. The strongest castles had walls over 1m thick. Rounded turrets at each corner gave defending archers a wide angle of fire.

Krak des Chevaliers was one of the most impregnable castles ever built. Its ruins stand in modern Syria.

LOP-SIDED
The Leaning Tower of Pisa was built in 1174 on soft ground and has been tilting over ever since.

FACTS AND FIGURES

Built in AD900, Ankhor Wat temple in Cambodia is the world's largest religious site.

The Egyptian, Imhotep, who lived in about 2600BC, is history's first known architect.

Rome's Colosseum, completed in AD80, could hold 50,000 spectators.

The Taj Mahal took 22 years to complete and needed up to 20,000 workers daily.

The Great Pyramid is 147m high and is built from about 2.3 million blocks of stone.

The defensive walls of Great Zimbabwe in southern Africa were 10m high and 5m thick.

The Blue Mosque in Istanbul, built 1550–57, has 400 tiny domes.

DATABANK

INPUT

Q Where is Stonehenge and when was it completed?

Q What was Rome's Colosseum used for?

Q When was Westminster Abbey in London built?

Q When were the first ever huts or houses built?

OUTPUT

A It was built from 3000–1800BC, in Wiltshire, UK.

A It was a stadium for bloody hand-to-hand combat.

A 1065. Rebuilt in 1245 by Henry II.

A About 35,000 years ago.

MARBLE MARVEL
India's most famous monument, the Taj Mahal was built in 1632–1649 by a Mogul emperor as a tomb for his beloved wife.

MODERN BUILDING

The use of steel and concrete has made the sky the limit for engineers of today, and gives architects greater freedom to experiment with unusual and breathtaking building designs.

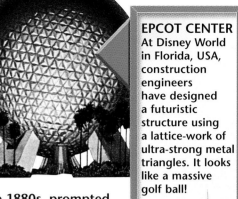

EPCOT CENTER
At Disney World in Florida, USA, construction engineers have designed a futuristic structure using a lattice-work of ultra-strong metal triangles. It looks like a massive golf ball!

Tallest building

The first 'skyscrapers' were built in Chicago, USA, during the 1880s, prompted by rising land prices. But it was in New York that the record-breakers were built. In 1930, the Chrysler Building topped the Eiffel Tower at 319m, and then a year later the Empire State Building soared to 381m. Not until 1973 was it overtaken by the World Trade Center, which stands 417m tall.

EVER UPWARD
Since the 1970s, engineers have pushed ever upwards – adding radio masts to achieve greater height.

Canary Wharf
244m
UK 1991

Bank of China
315m
Hong Kong 1988

Chrysler
Building
319m
USA 1930

John
Hancock
Center
343m
USA 1968

Empire
State
Building
381m
USA 1930

World Trade
Center
417m
USA 1973

Sears
Tower
443m
USA 1974

Petronas
Towers
451.9m
Malaysia
1996

CN
Tower
553.4m
Canada
1975

Bridges

The Romans were expert bridge builders and many of their aqueducts stand today. The Pont du Gard in France, built in AD14, is 250m long. Since then, longer and longer bridges have been attempted. When it was built in 1981, the Humber suspension bridge in the UK became the longest of its kind in the world, spanning 1,410m. It uses taut cables of many strands of steel to hold up its huge weight.

TAKING THE STRAIN
The Golden Gate Bridge in San Francisco, California, USA, is a suspension bridge. Built in 1937, it is 1,280m long.

FACTS AND FIGURES

The world's tallest radio mast is KTHI-TV Mast in Fargo, USA. It is 629m high.

The world's longest bridge is Pontchartrain Causeway in Lousiana. It is 38.4km long.

At 420m tall, Ekibastuz power station in Kazakhstan is the world's tallest chimney.

Petronas Towers in Malaysia are the world's tallest inhabited buildings.

Inspiration

In the 1950s, a competition was held to design a new arts centre for Sydney, Australia. It was won by Danish architect Jørn Urzon with his shell-like design inspired by South American temples and the boats in nearby Sydney harbour. Described as one of the seven wonders of the modern world, the Opera House was opened in 1973 and has attracted millions of visitors. Another innovative modern design is the Pompidou Centre in Paris, opened in 1977. The building's pipes, ducts, lifts, and supporting elements are all situated on the outside of the building and are very brightly coloured to draw attention to the remarkable structure. Today, it is one of the most famous cultural centres in the world.

HARD SHELL
The Opera House's roof 'shells' are made from sections of concrete covered with ceramic tiles.

Built in 1989, the Skydome stadium in Toronto, Canada, has the world's first fully retractable roof.

DATABANK

INPUT

Q What will be the world's tallest inhabited building by the year 2001?

Q How long is the longest tunnel in the world and when was it built?

Q Which cities in the world have the most skyscrapers over 152m?

OUTPUT

A The Shanghai World Financial Centre, begun in 1997, will be 460m high.

A The Seikan rail tunnel in Japan is 53.9km long and was completed in 1988.

A New York has 140; Chicago 68; Hong Kong and Houston both have 36.

UNDERSEA TRAVEL
Each of the Channel Tunnel's record-breaking twin rail tunnels is 49.94km long and has a diameter of 7.6m.

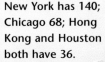

Channel Tunnel

A tunnel between England and France was planned over 200 years ago, but it was not until 1988 that it was started in earnest. Completed in 1994, the rail and service tunnels were dug by an Oahe-mole, a tungsten-tipped cutting machine. It moved a few metres per day lining the freshly excavated tunnels with concrete.

The first major traffic tunnel was built in the 1670s to carry the Canal du Midi in France. It was 158m long.

LASER-GUIDED
Tunnels were started in France and Britain simultaneously. Lasers ensured that the digging machines met in the middle.

ROAD AND RAIL

The wheel has been the most important technical innovation in human history. This simple device has been the basis for increasingly complicated modes of transport – taking us ever farther and faster.

On your bicycle

The first commercially successful bicycle, the velocipede, was built by France's Pierre Michaux in 1861. The bicycle is one of the most efficient forms of transport, and the most environmentally friendly. With little effort, and no pollution, cyclists can cruise at 16–24 km/h – up to five times walking pace.

FIRST CARS
The first cars were powered by steam. They needed constant refuelling and were slow and unreliable.

Over 21 million Volkswagen Beetles have been sold since their launch in 1937.

THRUSTING
Driven by Briton Richard Noble, *Thrust II* broke the 1,000 km/h barrier in 1983, at Black Rock Desert, USA.

The highway

The first motor car with a petrol engine was a three-wheeler built by Karl Benz in 1885. It was followed by fellow German Gottlieb Daimler's four-wheeled 'horseless carriage' in 1886. Early cars were expensive and it was not until the American company Oldsmobile introduced mass production around 1904 that they dropped in price. Later, also in the USA, Henry Ford installed moving assembly lines to speed up production still further. His Model T was designed as 'the family horse' and by 1920 accounted for around half the cars sold. Since then, the motor car has become the world's most popular form of transport.

In 1996, *Dream Solar*, a solar-powered car, covered 3,010km in 33.3 hours, averaging 85 km/h.

FREIGHT TRAIN
Australia is vast but lacks an extensive rail network. Instead, goods are transported by trucks that pull long trains of trailers.

DATABANK

Q What is the fastest public passenger train?

A The Japanese 'bullet train', which travels at an average speed of 261 km/h.

Q Where did the penny-farthing bicycle get its name from?

A Its wheels resembled the old British penny and farthing coins.

On track

The first steam railway engine was invented by England's Richard Trevithick in 1804. Intended as a cheap industrial transport, his engine carried 70 men and 10 tonnes of iron. In 1825, George Stephenson developed an engine to carry people on the first public railway between Stockton and Darlington in the UK. His *Rocket* had won the Rainhill trials, a national contest to find a reliable steam train for passenger travel. During the 1800s, steam railway spread throughout Europe and the US, with hundreds of new lines opening every year. In the 20th century, railways began searching for faster and more efficient alternatives to steam power. By 1939, the performance of the US-built Electro Motive over a range of slopes and conditions had sealed the fate of steam power. Today, high-speed trains, like the French TGV, have become the standard. In 1990, a modified TGV set a new rail record with a speed of 513 km/h. Despite this success, rail travel is in slow decline worldwide, as more people switch to cars and air travel.

GO WEST
Before the US rail network was built, colonists moving west in search of new lands travelled in long convoys. These massive 'wagon trains' made the hazardous journeys safer.

GREAT TRAIN
Der Adler was Germany's first steam railway engine. It was built by George Stephenson's son Robert in 1835.

FACTS AND FIGURES

The car *Thrust SSC* broke the land speed record in 1997, travelling at 1,227 km/h.

In 1938, *Mallard* became the world's fastest steam train, reaching speeds of 201 km/h.

The USA has over 6 million km of roads and freeways – more than any other country.

Citroën introduced the world's first front-wheel-drive car in 1934.

London has the oldest underground railway in the world. It opened in 1863.

MAGNETICS
The latest high-tech trains use high powered electro-magnets to float above special tracks. In tests in Germany, these futuristic trains have reached speeds of 436 km/h.

BOATS

The first primitive boats were made from fallen trees. Since then people have built bigger and better ships in order to cross rivers, seas and oceans to reach new lands.

Sailing by

Ancient stone tablets suggest that people were building boats as early as 4000BC. The funeral barge of the Egyptian Emperor Cheops, the earliest ship to be discovered, dates back to about 3000BC. Early Egyptian boats were powered almost entirely by oarsmen, with the later addition of a single square sail to harness wind power. The Arabs, using ships called *boums*, were the masters of wind power. They used lateen (triangle-shaped) sails that could be adjusted to make the most of any available wind. By the 15th century, European ships carried a combination of square and lateen sails, allowing them to trade with the far away lands of China and southeast Asia. As sea trade increased, so did fierce competition between sea-going nations. Many ships had to be armed with cannon for protection and this led to purpose-built warships and large navies.

Built in 1797, the warship *USS Constitution* survived many battles and is preserved to this day.

The first aircraft carriers were just old ships fitted with a flight deck to enable planes to land.

TEA CLIPPER
Designed in the USA, clippers were used to transport cargo quickly. One, the *Lightning*, had 10,869m² of sails, which enabled it to travel from Australia to the UK in 1854 in a record 64 days.

MERCHANT SHIPS
The prosperity of ancient Roman cities depended on trade ships to transport food, goods and armies to other ports.

FACTS AND FIGURES

Ken Warby reached 511 km/h on water in the hydroplane *Spirit of Australia* in 1978.

The first passenger-carrying liners operated across the Atlantic Ocean in the 1840s.

Ancient Greek trireme galleys used three rows of oarsmen to increase speed.

HMS Victory, moored in Portsmouth, UK, is the last ship-of-the-line on Earth.

Up to 7,800 people died when German liner *Wilhelm Gustloff* was torpedoed in 1945.

The first nuclear-powered submarine, the *Nautilus*, was launched in 1954.

NATIVE BOAT
The Dzelarhon native Americans used long and narrow vessels that were fast and easy to manoeuvre.

The nuclear-powered aircraft carrier, *USS Nimitz*, can sail around the world without refuelling.

Warships

By 1800, naval battles centred on ships-of-the-line, so-named because they would 'line' up alongside an enemy and fire as many cannon as possible into them. The most powerful held 100 cannon and could hit ships 500m away. In 1906, the Royal Navy unveiled the *Dreadnought*, a metal-hulled warship with guns that had a range of 15,000m. By the late-20th century, aircraft carriers and submarines carrying nuclear bombs had become the most important warships.

SUPER SUBMARINE
Modern submarines are nuclear-powered and operate at sea, undetected, for many months at a time.

Rudder

Nuclear reactor

Nuclear missiles

Living quarters

Torpedo chamber

Cargo carriers

Today, shipping is still the cheapest way to transport many goods around the world. Liquids such as oil are often transported in tankers, ships that get their name from the large tanks in which they carry their cargo. Other goods are carried on roll-on roll-off, or RoRo, ships. These vessels have openings, or ports, at both ends of the ship that allow vehicles to drive on and off when moving goods. The *Jahre Viking* is the largest cargo vessel in the world. It carries over 300,000 tonnes.

LEVIATHAN
Tankers are the biggest ships at sea. The largest petrol tankers can displace over 250,000 tonnes when full.

DATABANK

Q Which was the largest sailing ship in the world and what happened to it?

A The *France II* was 127m long and had five masts. Launched in 1911, it was wrecked in 1922.

Q Which was the biggest naval battle ever fought and who was involved?

A In 1916, 101 German and 151 British ships contested the Battle of Jutland.

Weird ships

Fishing boats catch over 100,000,000 tonnes of fish worldwide each year.

The idea that a ship could float on a cushion of air dates from 1877, but it was Christopher Cockerell, a British engineer, who patented the first practical hovercraft design in 1955. *SR.N1*, based on Cockerell's designs, was built four years later. The hydrofoil, first built in Italy by Enrico Forlanini in 1900, also appears to float above the sea. In reality, it has long, wing-like fins that force the ship upwards when travelling at high speeds.

IN THE AIR
The biggest hovercraft in the world, the *SR.N4 MkIII*, weighs 310 tonnes and is more than 56m long.

FLIGHT

Humans have often envied birds. The first attempts to match them were simple and unreliable, but today's planes have mastered the air.

Pioneers

In 1783, Joseph and Etienne Mongolfier of France launched the first manned balloon, proving that humans had the capability to defy gravity. Just over one hundred years later, Otto Lilienthal developed a primitive glider. In the USA, Orville and Wilbur Wright, encouraged by the newly invented petrol engine, built the first powered aeroplane, *Flyer 1*. In 1903, this fragile two-winged plane flew for just 36m, but it changed human history. By 1909, Frenchman Louis Blériot had built a plane powerful enough to fly the English Channel.

BIRD MAN
German inventor Otto Lilienthal studied bird flight in order to design his gliders. He crashed to his death in 1896.

Balloons are filled with gas or hot air. These are much lighter than the surrounding air, so they float.

STEALTHY DOES IT
The American F-117 'stealth' fighter is designed to be undetectable by enemy radar so it can bomb targets safely.

Cockpit

Cargo hold

Warplanes

The first aeroplanes were powered by propellers. They evolved quickly during World War I (1914–18) as each side built faster and more agile fighters to control the skies. World War II (1939–45) speeded up the development of jets, but the most crucial air battles were won by propeller-driven planes, such as the Spitfire, with its maximum speed of 710 km/h. Today, most warplanes are jet-powered and some travel faster than the speed of sound – about 1,200 km/h.

RED BARON
The triplane's three wings made it very manoeuverable during World War I air battles. It was favoured by Baron Manfred Von Richthoven of Germany, the war's finest pilot.

The Harrier Jump Jet uses its jets to rise straight up on take-off and does not need a runway.

FACTS AND FIGURES

Spanish engineer, Juan de la Cierva, built the autogyro (the first helicopter) in 1923.

The first trans-Atlantic flight took place in 1919 from Newfoundland to Portugal.

British engineer Frank Whittle designed the first jet engine in 1937.

Air travel

The jet engine enabled planes to fly further and faster. However, jets were thought to be uneconomical compared to piston engine aircraft for long-distance travel. In 1958, however, the first pure jet airliner, the 707, was launched and revolutionized aviation.

Tail fin

Rudder

Swept-back wings reduce air resistance

AIRLINER
Today there are about 950 Boeing 747s in the world. Many operate out of O'Hare Airport in Chicago, USA – the world's busiest airport. It deals with 66.5 million people a year.

Jet airliners proved cheap and easy to maintain. The 727 was launched in 1964 and, in 1970, the first jumbo jet, the 747, entered the skies. This could carry 560 people 8,000km without stopping. In 1976, Britain and France combined to build Concorde – a supersonic passenger plane. Carrying about 100 people each time, it cruises at up to 2,179 km/h.

Wing tip fin reduces air resistance

Engine

Fuel tanks

Engine

Due to their vulnerability, airliners are subject to more scrupulous safety checks than any other form of travel.

LIFE-SAVER
Helicopters have become an important part of everyday life – not least in rescuing people after accidents.

Disasters

Unlike most forms of travel, if an aeroplane develops a problem during flight, the consequences could easily be fatal. However, the worst air crash of all (below) took place in an airport. It was due to mistakes by the pilots and air traffic controllers. Other disasters have been caused by terrorists' bombs. In 1985, an Air India flight exploded over the Atlantic, killing the 329 people on board.

WORST EVER
On 27 March, 1977, two Boeing 747s collided at Los Rodeos Airport in Tenerife, Spain. 583 people died.

WEALTH AND RICHES

Money developed in early times as a more efficient way of trading goods and services than the simple act of swapping goods. Since then, it has become an important symbol of wealth, power, prestige and influence.

Money

In the ancient world, people traded one thing for another in a system known as barter, but there was no standard agreement on how much things were worth. Useful items, such as salt and daggers, became measures of value – as were ornamental objects, such as beads and seashells. The first true coins, made from silver and gold, date from the reign of King Croesus of Lydia (now part of present-day Turkey), around 650BC. Coins were popular because they were durable and easy to carry. Soon, city states all over nearby Greece were making their own coins.

MILITARY MONEY
By 1BC, campaigning Roman generals had begun to make their own coins in order to pay their soldiers in the field.

WORTHLESS
After defeat in World War I, Germany was forced to print so much money that its currency became utterly worthless. By November 1923, a loaf of bread cost over 200 billion marks.

The study of coins is called numismatics, and coin collectors are known as numismatists.

Richest countries

Countries measure their wealth in terms of Gross Domestic Product (GDP) per person. This is the value of all the goods and services produced within a country's borders each year, divided by its population. According to a 1997 United Nations survey, Luxembourg has the highest GDP at $37,785 per person. The lowest belongs to the Democratic Republic of Congo, which has a GDP of just $52 per person – over 726 times less than that of Luxembourg.

RICH DESERTS
Once very poor, Saudi Arabia became hugely rich after the exploitation of its massive oil reserves.

The Bank of England was founded in 1694 for the sole purpose of raising money for wars.

TRADE CENTRE
Following the devastating stock market crash of 1929, the New York Stock Exchange, in Wall Street, recovered to become one of the world's most important financial centres.

DATABANK
INPUT

Q What is the biggest gambling win ever seen and where did it take place?

Q Which country produces the most gold in the world and how much does it produce?

Q What is the euro, who uses it and when was it introduced?

Q What and where is Fort Knox – and why is it famous?

Super-rich

The richest man in the world is probably William 'Bill' Gates III who, in 1999, was estimated to be worth as much as $90 billion. Gates's wealth is based on the software company Microsoft, which he formed in 1975. He is now richer than the oil and gas magnate, the Sultan of Brunei, who was previously the world's wealthiest man. One of the super-rich of the 19th century was John Davison Rockefeller, an oil tycoon who founded the Standard Oil Company in 1870. His company gave him control of the US oil trade – and earned him a vast amount of money. Rockefeller became a great philanthropist, giving over $500 million to charity before his death in 1937. His personal fortune, estimated at $1.4 billion, was inherited by his son, John D. Rockefeller Jr.

The richest person in the ancient world was Croesus of Lydia. His wealth was the source of legends.

FACTS AND FIGURES

There are over 8.7 billion one-dollar bills in circulation in the USA.

Rogue trader, Nick Leeson, lost over $800 million when he bankrupted Barings Bank.

At the tender age of three, Athina Roussel inherited a $5 billion business empire.

Bahrain and Quatar are so rich that they have an income tax rate of zero per cent.

Warren Buffet is the richest stock market trader, with a fortune of over $15 billion.

OIL SULTAN
One of the richest men in the world is Muda Hassan al Bolkiah Mu'izz-ud-Din-Wad-daulah, Sultan of Brunei, whose wealth derives from his country's natural resources.

RICH ROYALTY
The Queen's personal fortune of £450 million does not include the Crown Jewels and land that comes with her title.

BILLIONAIRE
William Gates III first started programming computers at the age of 13 and left university to found his own company. Today, his wealth is greater than that of many countries.

OUTPUT

A Two lucky winners from Wisconsin, USA, won over $110 million on the Powerball Lottery in 1993.

A South Africa, which produced nearly 500 tonnes in 1996, is the largest gold producer in the world.

A Adopted in 1999, the euro is the common currency for members of the European Union.

A Fort Knox is an army base famed for housing the US gold reserve and the US constitution during World War II.

PRECIOUS OBJECTS

Diamonds and finely crafted gold jewellery are valued for their beauty, yet some objects are precious because they are rare, strange or have a religious significance. Each culture places value on different items.

Gems and jewels

Gems, such as diamonds and rubies, occur naturally and are valued for their rarity and beauty. The largest diamond found was the Cullinan. It measured 10 x 6.5 x 5cm. Presented to King Edward VII, it was cut into smaller gems, which now adorn the British Crown Jewels. Pearls, made by humble oysters, are also greatly treasured.

Jewellers cut large natural diamonds into smaller stones to improve their quality.

TOP HAT
Crown jewels symbolized a monarch's power. They were worn to impress subjects and enemies.

Buried treasure

While excavating Troy in Turkey in the 1870s, German Heinrich Schliemann found a great treasure hoard. He identified it as belonging to Troy's legendary king, Priam. Other major finds include the Dead Sea Scrolls in Israel, 1947. One famous treasure eludes all – the Holy Grail. It is said to be the cup used by Jesus at the Last Supper.

RESCUED FROM THE DEPTHS
Objects recovered from shipwrecks, such as the *Mary Rose* which sank in 1545, help historians to understand the past.

TREASURE OF THE PHARAOHS
Tutankhamun's tomb was only discovered in 1922. It contained fabulous treasures, such as the death-mask of the pharaoh.

DATABANK

INPUT	OUTPUT
Q What is the hardest gemstone in the world?	**A** Diamonds are the hardest naturally occuring substance on Earth.
Q What happens if I find some old jewellery lying in a field? Can I keep it?	**A** In some countries, any find is called treasure trove and becomes state property!
Q Why are people prepared to pay so much for old pictures or antiques?	**A** Collectors are usually attracted by an object's age, rarity and unique qualities.

Collectables

Works by respected artists, such as Fabergé, Picasso and Van Gogh, are guaranteed to sell for many millions of pounds or dollars. Some objects are valuable for less obvious reasons. Rare children's toys, such as early teddy bears, are eagerly sought. In 1994, a collector paid £12,650 for a toy van that was made in 1937. A famous person's belongings may also be valuable. President J. F. Kennedy's comb was sold for over $1,000, while the birth certificate of famous singer Paul McCartney fetched $84,146.

Karl Fabergé created beautiful eggs from precious metals and gems for the Russian Imperial Family.

RARE STAMP
Old and unusual stamps, such as the Penny Black – the first ever stamp – are highly prized by collectors.

SUNFLOWERS
Van Gogh's *Sunflowers* made £22.5 million at auction in 1987. However, rumours suggest that it is a fake.

HEADS
Coins were once made from precious metals. Today, such coins are worth far more than their face value!

TOMB RAIDER
Many treasures of Ancient Egypt were stolen by grave robbers. Gold statues were melted down and sold.

Theft and thieves

Wherever there are precious objects, there will be people aiming to steal them. The fabled Amber Room of the Catherine Palace, Russia, was removed by German soldiers on Hitler's orders in 1945 and has vanished. A single panel mysteriously reappeared in 1997. Edvard Munch's famous painting *The Scream* was stolen from Norway's National Art Gallery in 1994. Luckily, it was recovered soon after.

VIKING RAID
In the past, in times of war, people often hid or buried their valuables. Such hoards are still being uncovered today.

ART

A work of art is how an artist interprets honestly what they see or feel. Art can take many different forms, two of which are painting and sculpture.

Early art

The Ancient Greeks were the first people to see art as a pleasure rather than as a homage to the gods. But early European art reverted to religious images, in the form of Biblical illustrations (above), such as the *Lindisfarne Gospels* (AD700). With Islam, human images were taboo, but abstract art flourished. It reached its peak in the building of the Alhambra Palace in Granada, Spain, 1338–90. Its beauty prevented conquering Christian monarchs from destroying it!

ILLUSTRATED MANUSCRIPT
In medieval art, the religious message was more important than the accuracy of the figures in the painting.

FACTS AND FIGURES

Masaccio's *Holy Trinity*, painted in 1427, is the first example of perspective in art.

A set of 356 cone sculptures, called *Desert Breath*, covers 10 hectares of Egypt's desert.

Made in 1080 in Normandy, the hand-stitched Bayeux Tapestry is 70m long.

The Post-impressionist artist Paul Cézanne is regarded as the father of modern art.

Thousands of paintings have vanished without trace – including 350 by Picasso.

The earliest examples of art are cave paintings from about 40,000 years ago.

Renaissance

Renaissance means 'rebirth' and refers to the period 1350–1550 when Italian artists in particular tried to revive the glory of Ancient Greek and Roman art. Artists such as Botticelli, Raphael and Leonardo da Vinci took art to a higher plane, using perspective and depth to add realism to their art. One of the most celebrated artists of the age was Michelangelo. He was master of the human form, as is shown in his sculpture *David* and the painting *The Creation of Adam* (below). He was also an architect.

Renaissance artists succeeded in making their subjects look natural – a revolution at that time!

MICHELANGELO'S MASTERPIECE
Michelangelo frescos, painted from 1508–12 on the ceiling of the Sistine Chapel, Rome, are among his best works.

Impressionism

Towards the end of the 19th century, some French artists evolved a new style of painting. People like Manet, Monet and Seurat wanted to portray life in a fresh way, conveying an 'impression' of a scene rather than painting it in detail. They experimented widely with light, colour and texture. Their work influenced artists all over the world to paint in a freer, livelier way.

The Impressionists were followed by the Post-impressionists, who wanted to give art more solidity.

SUNDAY AFTERNOON
Georges Seurat (1859–91) built up his pictures from tiny dots of paint. His style gives an 'impression' of a scene.

Modern art

The Impressionists' new approach led many artists to reject the ideas of the past. Instead of showing life as we see it, they became ever more experimental. Vincent Van Gogh (1853–90) used colour and form to convey what he felt about the things he painted. Pablo Picasso (1881–1973) tested how far he could go in painting abstract images of everyday objects. Piet Mondrian (1872–1944) built pictures out of straight lines and colours. Such ideas consistently scandalized the art critics of their time. Even today, challenging works by leading artists, such as Damian Hirst, draw as much criticism as they do praise.

In 1991, Damian Hirst held an exhibition which included an entire dead shark preserved in a tank.

POP ART
Andy Warhol (1926–87) was the pioneer of pop art, which linked art and popular culture with paintings of cola bottles and soup cans. He filmed over 6,000 hours of his own life.

DATABANK

Q What is considered to be the most valuable painting in the world?

A *Mona Lisa* (1502) by da Vinci. It is considered priceless but in 1963 was valued at £35 million.

Q Which are Europe's most famous art galleries and where are they?

A They include the Louvre, Paris, France; Uffizi, Florence, Italy; and Prado, Madrid, Spain.

THE WRITTEN WORD

The first stories were passed on orally, but with the invention of writing and later printing, the written word became a universal means of sharing profound ideas.

THE PRINTING PRESS
German Johann Gutenberg invented the printing press in 1455. It enabled exact copies to be made of text and images.

Printing

Before printing, books had to be copied by hand – so few were made! The Chinese first used printed type in the 11th century, but it was another 400 years before the technique appeared in Europe. By the 18th century, presses could print 1,000 pages an hour and newspapers and books became available to everyone.

In 1517, Martin Luther used mass-produced leaflets to spread his rebellion against the Church.

One of the earliest novels is *The Tale of Genji* written by Japan's Lady Murasaki Shikibu in the 11th century.

DOMESDAY BOOK
William the Conqueror's painstaking survey of England in 1086 is one of history's greatest surviving records.

FACTS AND FIGURES

The Library of Congress, Washington, DC, in the USA holds over 23 million books.

The oldest handwritten copy of the Qur'an dates from AD1091 from Bangladesh.

The novelist George Eliot (1819–80) was really a woman called Mary Ann Evans!

The great poem *The Epic of Gilgamesh*, from Sumeria (Turkey), dates from 2000BC.

Pencils date from the 1490s. Hungarian Laslo Biro invented the ball-point pen in 1938.

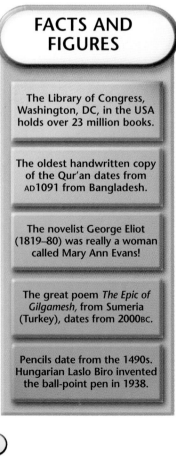

THE WIZARD OF OZ
The Wizard of Oz was the first of 14 books about the magical world of Oz by American author L. Frank Baum.

Books for kids

Once upon a time it was thought that children's books should offer stern moral lessons and little else. By the 19th century however, Mark Twain's *Adventures of Tom Sawyer* (1876) and Rudyard Kipling's *The Jungle Book* (1894) offered more exciting reading. The first modern picture book was Beatrix Potter's *Tale of Peter Rabbit* (1900). It was followed by A. A. Milne's *Winnie-the-Pooh* in 1926, enhanced by illustrations by Ernest Shepherd. Today, the *Harry Potter* novels by J. K. Rowling are a great favourite with children around the world.

J.K. ROWLING

HARRY POTTER

JUNIOR WIZARD
After discovering that he is a wizard, Harry Potter goes to the wizard school Hogwarts where he has many adventures.

Drama

Before television and film, theatre provided public entertainment. In the Middle Ages, plays had a religious theme, but later the subject matter broadened. In Britain, men such as William Congreve and Ben Jonson followed Shakespeare in writing comedies or tragedies to capture public imagination.

Great modern playwrights include Russia's Anton Checkov, and Ireland's Sean O'Casey and Samuel Beckett.

THE BARD
Shakespeare's plays used to be performed in intimate London playhouses such as the *Globe* or the *Rose*.

Poetry

French poet Paul Valéry described prose as walking and poetry dancing! Poetry expresses experiences or emotions in words arranged for their rhythm and sound. Rhyming verses are also important. It is an ancient art and was used by the writer of the *Iliad* (800–700BC) – the epic of the Trojan War. Modern poets use poetry to describe anything from heaven and hell to the health of a pet goldfish!

Novels

A novel explores human life using characters and a storyline. Novels gained importance in the 18th century and later became popular with the works of France's Victor Hugo, Russia's Leo Tolstoy and Britain's Charles Dickens. There are many types of novel. Raymond Chandler and Agatha Christie wrote about crime, Isaac Asimov is famous for science fiction, while J. R. R. Tolkien's *Lord of the Rings* is an epic fantasy fairy tale.

CERVANTES
The Spanish writer Miguel de Cervantes wrote *Don Quixote* in 1605 – one of the first novels. It follows the adventures of the hapless hero who wants to be a chivalrous knight of old.

Comic books

A comic is a series of pictures and words that tell a story. Early comics got their name from the funny stories they told. In the US, comic books became popular with the creation of the superhero *Superman* in the 1930s. Many early comics like the UK's *The Dandy* (1937) and *The Beano* (1938) are still popular today with children.

Tintin is one of the most famous comic characters. He was created by the Belgian Hergé in 1929.

LEGENDARY DARK KNIGHT
Created by Bob Kane, the popular character Batman first appeared in *Detective Comics 27* in May 1939.

MUSIC

From simple prehistoric drums to the computerized dance tunes of the 1990s, music has played a vital part in almost every human culture.

In John Cage's *4'33"*, the performers sit in silence and the 'music' is any noise made by the audience.

Early music

Pipes and drums have been found among the remains of the earliest settlements. Drums and string instruments, such as the harp, may have evolved from beating cooking pots and twanging the strings of hunting bows. The Ancient Egyptians, Chinese, Romans and Greeks were all sophisticated singers and musicians but the earliest piece of music found to date is a hymn from Sumeria (present-day Iraq) from about 700BC.

SOUND OF THE SOUTH
Invented by Australian aborigines, the didgeridoo is a wind instrument that has a unique, haunting tone.

Despite his fame and talent, Mozart died penniless at the age of 35 and was buried in an unmarked grave.

Classical music

Classical and baroque music began in the Middle Ages in Italy and so most musical terms are Italian. Yet music was taken to greater heights by German composers, such as Johann Sebastian Bach (1685–1750) – regarded by many as the most accomplished musician ever. The child prodigy, Mozart (1756–91), developed musical styles further, writing 27 piano concertos. Ludwig van Beethoven (1770–1827) pioneered the 'romantic' style, and continues to influence classical music today. The 20th century has seen the rise of recorded music – bringing classical music into the home.

PIANOFORTE
The piano was invented in Italy in 1709. Its full name describes how it plays notes both loudly and softly.

YOU WHAT?
Although he did not become totally deaf until 1819, Beethoven wrote much of his music, including his famous *Fifth Symphony*, while his hearing was severely impaired.

FACTS AND FIGURES

Candle in the Wind by Elton John, with sales of 35 million, is the best-selling single ever.

The earliest organ, the Ancient Greek hydraulus, dates from about 230BC.

Wolfgang Amadeus Mozart had written 200 musical works by the age of 18.

Jimmy Osmond was only nine years old when he had a UK No.1 hit in 1972.

As many as 3.5 million people saw Rod Stewart's concert in Rio de Janeiro, Brazil, 1994.

The biggest-earning boy band in the world were New Kids on the Block from the USA.

DATABANK

INPUT

Q Which musical instruments are known as woodwind instruments?

Q What is opera and where does it originate from?

Q Who was the first rock 'n' roll singer or band – and what was their first song?

Q What is soul music and who are the greatest soul singers?

MUSICAL YOUTHS
The Spice Girls' first six singles went to No. 1 in the UK charts. The album *Spice* is the best-selling album by a British act.

Rock and pop

Elvis Presley (1935–77) brought rock 'n' roll to the masses with hits such as *Love Me Tender* and *Heartbreak Hotel*. He had a total of 18 No. 1 singles and nine No.1 albums in the USA. Elvis was followed in the 1960s by groups like Mick Jagger's Rolling Stones and The Beatles led by Paul McCartney and John Lennon. The Beatles' album *Sgt Pepper's Lonely Hearts Club Band* is thought by many to be the greatest album of all time. However, the best-selling album is *Thriller* by Michael Jackson, which was released in 1982 and has sold over 45 million copies globally. The biggest selling bands of the 1990s include Take That, Oasis, the Spice Girls and Boyzone.

ROLLING ON
The Rolling Stones had their first hit in 1963 and were still releasing singles in the late 1990s.

It was not until Columbia Records introduced the long-play record in 1948 that albums could be made.

SUPERSTAR
Madonna's first major hit was *Holiday*, released in 1982. Since then she has become a global superstar.

Jazz and blues

Jazz is a blend of African musical traditions with European folk and classical styles. It first emerged at the end of the 19th century among the marching bands of southern US cities such as New Orleans. Two of the greatest jazz musicians were Louis Armstrong and Duke Ellington. The Blues also evolved in the southern US states. Its roots lie in West African music and work-songs.

OUTPUT

A The flute, oboe, piccolo, clarinet, bassoon and recorder are woodwind instruments.

A Opera could be described as theatre and poetry set to music. It originated in Italy in the 17th century.

A Bill Haley and His Comets are regarded as the first. Their first single, *Rock Around the Clock*, was released in 1955.

A Soul grew out of African–American gospel music. Singers include Aretha Franklin and James Brown.

THAT'S JAZZ
Jazz was the 'pop' music of the first half of the 20th century. Jazz clubs are still extremely popular today.

CINEMA

The major art form of the 20th century, moving pictures or 'movies' are made primarily to entertain audiences, but are also a record of our ever-changing world.

SCREEN IDOL
Greta Garbo (1905–90) was a great star of silent films and talkies. She lived as a recluse from 1941 onwards.

Silent era

The first film-makers experimented with sound, yet films were silent until 1927. One of the earliest films, *The Great Train Robbery* (1903), was also the first western. It lasted just ten minutes. Big studios relied on major stars, such as Mary Pickford, to bring in audiences. The most famous of all was comic Charlie Chaplin.

In 1896, *The Kiss Between May Irvin and John C. Rice* showed cinema's first screen kiss.

WARNER BROS · SUPREME TRIUMPH
AL JOLSON
JAZZ SINGER

TALKIE TIME
The first film with sound was *The Jazz Singer* (1927), starring Al Jolson. It was also the first musical.

Hollywood

The traditional home of the film industry, the Hollywood legend began when a group of film producers moved to the Los Angeles suburb just before World War I. The studios they founded, including Fox and Metro-Goldwyn-Mayer, controlled movie-making by the 1930s, and turned it into a million-dollar business. Hollywood is still a major centre for film-making.

SOME LIKE IT HOT
Marilyn Monroe (1926–62) was, for many, the ultimate Hollywood icon. She died of an overdose of sleeping pills.

FACTS AND FIGURES

In 1895, the Lumière brothers were the first to show films to paying customers.

Titanic (1997), is the most expensive film ever made. It cost $200 million.

Ben-Hur (silent, 1925) cost $4 million to make. The 1959 remake cost $14.5 million.

Over 300 films have been made worldwide of the plays of William Shakespeare.

India produces more films than any other country – with a peak of 948 films in 1990.

The longest film of all time is the 85–hour long *Cure For Insomnia* (1987).

The British film *Gandhi* (1982) used 300,000 extras during filming.

The character Sherlock Holmes has been portrayed by 75 actors in 211 films.

LIGHTS! CAMERA! ACTION!
Film producers and directors originally moved to Hollywood because of the pleasant climate and wide open spaces.

DATABANK

INPUT

 Q When did colour films start to replace black and white?

 Q Which film has won the most Academy Awards (Oscars)?

Q Which country's people go to the cinema most often?

Q Which is regarded as the best film of all time?

OUTPUT

 A Colour was first used in 1894, but only took over in the late 1960s.

 A *Ben-Hur* (1959) and *Titanic* (1997) both won 11 Oscars.

A Lebanese people go to the cinema over 35 times a year each!

A Experts list *Citizen Kane* (1941); film lovers say *Casablanca* (1943)!

USE THE FORCE
The Empire Strikes Back (1980) was the second *Star Wars* film. The series is the most successful in cinema history.

PROFITS UP AS SHIP GOES DOWN
The highest grossing film ever made is Titanic (1997). By 1999, it had made $1,600 million in profits.

Blockbusters

Hollywood's success since 1945 has rested partly on big budget films packed with stars. Using special effects, huge sets and exotic locations, these films are expensive, and not all make money. *Cutthroat Island* (1995) had losses of $80 million! One of the most successful series has been the *Indiana Jones* trilogy, starring Harrison Ford and directed by Steven Spielberg. Ford also starred in three *Star Wars* films. Other blockbusters include the *Batman* series and *Men in Black* (1997) starring Will Smith.

If inflation is taken into account, *Gone With the Wind* (1939) would be the highest grossing film ever.

SCHINDLER'S LIST
Steven Spielberg's film about the German who saved the lives of his Jewish workers in World War II won seven Oscars in 1993.

Directors

Film direction is a highly regarded art. Alfred Hitchcock was expert at portraying suspense, while Stanley Kubrick was famous for his visual extravaganzas and attention to detail. Several actors, including Clint Eastwood and Robert Redford, are also film directors. Orson Welles managed to direct and star in *Citizen Kane* (1941). Quentin Tarantino, who directed *Reservoir Dogs* (1992) and *Pulp Fiction* (1994), is one of today's most popular directors.

FOOD AND DRINK

Food and drink are vital for life, yet what we eat depends on many factors, such as our religion or where we live. Some rare foods have become much sought-after luxuries.

Farming

In developed countries, such as the UK and USA, machinery and large farms mean that farming is big business. In poorer areas, farming is small-scale, providing enough food only for the farmer and his family. Cereals such as wheat, maize and rice are the most commonly cultivated foods and make up half the world's food intake. Animal farming for meat, milk, wool and leather is also vitally important. The world's most widely drunk beverage is tea, made from a plant cultivated in China and India since the 3rd century AD. Coffee was first drunk in Ethiopia in the 15th century. As it became popular in Europe, the plant was taken to Brazil and the Caribbean where it is now farmed on a massive scale.

SWEET CROP
Sugar cane is the main source of sugar. It originates from Pacific islands. Sugar is also extracted from sugar beet.

PADDY FIELDS
Rice is the main crop of countries such as China and India. It is grown in flooded fields to take advantage of seasonal rain.

In the USA today, farming employs three per cent of workers compared to 90 per cent 200 years ago.

BANANA REPUBLIC
Bananas are one of the most popular and nutritious tropical fruits. A single bunch can hold up to 150 bananas.

FACTS AND FIGURES

Across the world more people work in farming than in all other occupations combined.

In the UK, 700 million chickens are eaten each year, – more than ten per person.

Instant coffee is strong liquid coffee that has been freeze-dried.

Saturated fat, found in meat and dairy foods, should only be 10 per cent of an ideal diet.

The Australians are the biggest consumers of meat per person.

A cake preserved in an Egyptian tomb is thought to be about 4,200 years old.

Wild ginseng, a rare spice found in China, sells for up to £310,000 per gramme.

MECHANIZED FARMING
Machines such as the combine harvester make it easy for a handful of workers to farm an enormous area.

What we eat

A balanced diet provides us with energy for our activities and with the material the body needs to grow and repair itself. Different cultures have distinctive diets. Developed nations eat more meat than is healthy, while Hindus in India view animals as sacred and so eat vegetables only. A Mediterranean diet centres on seafood, fruit and vegetables while Asian cultures often cook with spices.

SHARK'S FIN
Shark's fin soup is so popular in many Asian countries that sharks are disappearing as a result.

HAMBURGER
The typical food item of the USA, the hamburger was introduced by German immigrants in the 19th century.

SPICE SALE
Spices play a vital part in Eastern cooking. Rare spices, such as saffron or wild ginseng, are very expensive.

Strange tastes

Food and drink are a basic requirement for life, yet some have acquired a mystique based on rarity and flavour that makes them very expensive. These include Kopi Luwak, an Indonesian coffee. The beans are collected from the droppings of palm civets before being roasted. The civet's digestive system seems to give the coffee extra flavour! In Spain, fishermen brave raging storms merely to catch a rare barnacle. In southeastern Asia, particularly in Thailand, people risk their lives to collect swiftlet nests from sea caves. Constructed from the bird's saliva, the nests are prized by chefs who make soup from them. Nests are advertized on the Internet for $2,000–12,000 per kg.

TRUFFLES
Truffles are a type of rare fungus. They are expensive because they are difficult to find and even harder to grow. A white species from Italy sells for over £11,500 per kg.

CHOCOLATE
When chocolate first reached Europe from Mexico in the 1600s, only the wealthy could afford it.

EGG BOXES
Caviar is the eggs of the sturgeon, a type of fish. Most comes from Russia. The rarest type costs £625 per 50g.

GOOD PLONK
The most expensive bottle of wine was a Château Lafite from 1787. It was sold in 1985 for £105,000.

Truffle hunters in Europe use specially trained dogs or even pigs to find the precious fungus.

RUSSIAN CAVIAR
net wt 4.13 (4.oz)
Produced and packed for export
CASPIAN CAVIAR BALYKCORPORATION
KASPRYBA ASTRAKHAN

CAVIAR
PRODUCT OF THE CASPIAN SEA

RUSSIAN CAVIAR
Produced and packed in Russia only for export

CAVIAR

Vin de

89

THE FUTURE

The last 1,000 years have seen many changes to the way we live, particularly the last few decades. The future looks equally exciting – but only if we are prepared to look after our world.

TAKING OVER
Robots are becoming more intelligent. An American robot is being developed that can hear, speak, feel and even think!

Home comforts

Houses are being built with Internet connections in every room, enabling you to operate appliances from an office on the other side of the world. You can even water your garden while you are on holiday! Houses will also be fitted with devices like 'intelligent' smoke alarms. These switch off gas or electricity if they detect a problem.

ELECTRIC CAR
To cope with an ever-rising population, transport of the future must be cleaner and more efficient.

Scientists are able to clone animals. Many people are worried about the prospect of cloning humans.

Genetics

By manipulating genes, scientists alter animals and plants for our benefit. Some would like to experiment on humans in order to combat disease and even remove unpleasant character traits! It will soon be possible to clone human organs so that each person would have spares stored for future transplants.

WIND FARM
Extraordinary sights, such as this wind farm, may one day become common in the quest for new power.

Power

Electricity may become the chief power of the future. Today it is produced by burning coal, oil or gas in power stations, yet reserves of oil are expected to run out by 2030 and coal by 2200. Nuclear power stations are also in decline – the risks heavily outweigh the benefits. Most experts think wind, tidal or solar power will be the future.

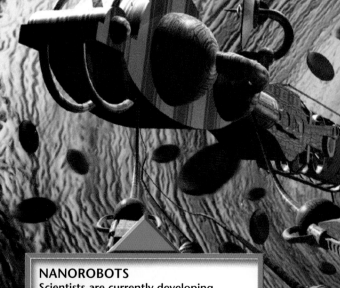

NANOROBOTS
Scientists are currently developing machines small enough to travel through the bloodstream and repair any damage.

New homes

The new millennium could witness a
permanent human settlement on the
Moon. It would become a scientific
research base and provide living space
for thousands of people. The Moon may
also be a valuable
stepping stone for
missions to Mars. A
few experts believe
that the red planet
could be turned
into a new
Earth!

FACTS AND FIGURES

Machines which identify
people by scanning their eyes
will be common by 2010.

By 2010, most houses will
have robots as pets, which
may even do all the chores!

Cash will soon be replaced
with ultra-safe and easy to
carry 'smart' cards.

By the year 2030, robots
may outnumber humans
in developed countries.

Some experts believe that
nanorobots will be in use by
the year 2015.

LIFE ON MARS
A Mars mission
may take place
by 2030. The
journey will take
up to a year, so,
after creating
a base, the
astronauts will
need to process
fuel from the
planet for their
return journey.

The end?

Since the invention of atom bombs, we have become
aware of how easy it is to destroy life on Earth.
Global warming may melt the ice caps, turning
the planet into a big ocean. Pollution could
poison the land so that we cannot
grow any food. Yet many experts
believe that we will colonize
other planets – and
create new worlds.

SPLAT!
Space contains
millions of huge
asteroids, and
many have hit
Earth in the
past. Should
one strike Earth
in the near
future we could
be wiped out,
just as the
dinosaurs were.

GLOSSARY

This section explains some of the more unusual or difficult terms that have been used in this book. The entries are arranged in alphabetical order.

FORCE
The Shuttle's rockets provide a thrusting force that enables it to escape the pulling force of Earth's gravity.

Astrology The belief that the positions and movements of planets and stars have an influence on human affairs.

Astronomy The scientific study of Space and everything within it.

Atom Tiny particles that make up all the matter in the Universe. Splitting atoms are central to nuclear reactions.

Big Bang The theory that the Universe began as a minute ball of matter, which exploded and formed all of the planets, stars and galaxies.

Black hole When a large star uses up all its fuel, it collapses in upon itself creating a black hole. A black hole has a huge gravitational pull and attracts all other objects, including light, towards it.

Climate A region's weather measured over a long period of time. Climate is influenced by factors such as how close the area is to the Equator, an ocean or a mountain range.

Communism A system of political and economic organization where the people in a community share the community's wealth according to their need.

WAR
A state of war exists when hostility between nations or groups of people escalates into armed conflict.

Forms of communism were used in the former USSR (Russia and its republics) and eastern Europe until the early 1990s. It survives in China and Cuba.

Developed countries This term is used to describe the wealthy, industrial nations of the world. These include the USA, Japan and western European countries.

Eclipse This occurs when a planet or moon moves into the shadow of another. On Earth, a solar eclipse occurs when the Moon's shadow falls on part of Earth, creating a period of darkness during the day.

Element An element, such as oxygen, gold or carbon, is a basic substance that cannot be broken down into other substances. Each contains just one type of atom.

Environment Earth and everything within in it, including plants, animals, people, the air around us and the soil beneath our feet. Our destruction of parts of the environment threatens Earth's future.

Fascism The belief that the state is more important than individuals and that all citizens must obey their leader. Fascism took hold in parts of Europe after World War I, particularly in Italy and Germany. Adolf Hitler's Nazi party used Fascism to gain and hold power in Germany through violence and intimidation.

Fossil Remains of an animal or plant preserved in rock. Over long periods of time, a fossil becomes part of the rock itself or just an impression in rock.

Galaxy A group of stars held together by their own gravity. There are thought to be billions of galaxies in the Universe, each containing millions of stars. Our galaxy is called the Milky Way.

Genetics The study of how organisms pass on characteristics to their offspring. Genes are the molecules within the body that contain the inherited information.

Gravity The force of attraction between objects. The larger the object and the closer you are to it, the greater the force you feel. For example, Earth exerts a strong pull on everything on its surface.

Invertebrate Any animal that does not have a backbone. Includes insects, arachnids, crustaceans, worms, molluscs and jellyfish.

Middle Ages An era of history – also known as the medieval period – that began with the fall of the Roman Empire in about AD500 and ended in about AD1450–80.

Millennium One thousand years of history.

Nuclear reaction By splitting atoms, scientists release a vast amount of energy. This nuclear power is used to produce electricity and is the basis for atom bombs.

Organism Any living thing, including all plants and animals.

Prehistoric A term referring to the history of the world before humans began making written records (about 3000BC).

Religion The belief in God or gods – who are usually entitled to obedience and worship. Major religions include Judaism, Buddhism, Islam, Christianity and Hinduism.

Renaissance A movement in art, literature and science that took place from about 1350 to 1550 based on a revival of ancient learning. It began in Italy.

Revolution The overthrow of a government by its subjects. Revolutions have occurred in many countries including France (1789) and Russia (1917).

Universe Encompasses everything that exists – from the largest galaxy in Space to the tiniest particle of an atom on a pinhead. The Universe is unimaginably large.

Vertebrate Any animal with a backbone, such as fish, amphibians, reptiles, birds and mammals.

MAMMAL
Animals that can control their own body temperature and are usually covered in hair or fur. Most give birth instead of laying eggs and all produce milk to feed their growing young.

INDEX